HIGHER
English

grade booster

David Cockburn

Text © 2005 David Cockburn
Design and layout © 2005 Leckie & Leckie Ltd
Cover image © Caleb Rutherford

1st edition printed 2005

All rights reserved. No part of this publication may be reproduced, stored in a retrieval system, or transmitted in any form or by any means, electronic, mechanical, photocopying, recording or otherwise, without the prior permission in writing from Leckie & Leckie Ltd. Legal action will be taken by Leckie & Leckie Ltd against any infringement of our copyright.

ISBN 1-84372-259-3

Published by
Leckie & Leckie Ltd, 8 Whitehill Terrace, St Andrews, Scotland KY16 8RN
tel: 01334 475656 fax: 01334 477392
enquiries@leckieandleckie.co.uk www.leckieandleckie.co.uk

Special thanks to
Larry Flanagan (content review), Andrew Foley (illustration),
The Partnership Publishing Solutions Ltd (design and page make-up),
Roda Morrison (copy-editing) and Caleb Rutherford (cover design).

A CIP Catalogue record for this book is available from the British Library.

Leckie & Leckie is a division of Granada Learning Limited, part of ITV plc.

CONTENTS

1. Higher English Language Skills 5
2. The Origins of English 13
3. What is Grammar? 19
4. Subordinate Clauses 24
5. Analysing the Words 27
6. Sentence Structure 38
7. Further Features of Sentence Structure 43
8. Punctuation 53
9. Imagery, Word Choice, Tone and Conclusions 67
10. Literary Devices 80
11. Meaning 87
12. Textual Analysis 97
13. The Critical Essay – Narrative Structure 106
14. Personal Study and Critical Essays – *What you have to do* 117
15. The Personal Study and Critical Essays – *The importance of accuracy* 124
16. Your Own Writing 129
17. Avoid These Mistakes 137

   Conclusion 144
   Answers 145
   Glossary 151

1 Higher English Language Skills

Why do I need this book?

What will I learn?

The coursework and the examination

An example of essential key skills: word order

Exam example

What is grammar?

WHY DO I NEED THIS BOOK?

This book will teach you all the language skills you need for your Higher English coursework and for the Higher examination itself. To many people the word 'language' can be confusing: does it refer to the French language? Or the German? Or Latin? What exactly is meant by 'English language'?

The term 'language' as it is used in this book – and in your Higher coursework and in the examination – refers to every aspect of the English language: from **words**, themselves, to **sentence structure**, to **punctuation**, to **paragraphs**, to the **way paragraphs are linked**, to **narrative structure**, to **imagery** and other **literary devices**. Don't worry if some of these terms are unfamiliar to you at the moment – you will be entirely familiar with them by the end of this book. If the term is followed by a key symbol, then, for quick reference, you can find a definition in the glossary at the end of the book.

WHAT WILL I LEARN?

It is the purpose of this book to give you all the knowledge and skills you need to do well in Higher English. You will learn how to answer the questions about language that crop up in Close Reading and Textual Analysis. You will learn how to analyse and evaluate linguistic and literary techniques and, in addition, you will learn how to write appropriately and effectively in your coursework and in the exam itself. Reading and writing are closely related: the more you develop your reading skills, the more your writing skills improve as you adopt the techniques learned in developing those reading skills; and as you develop your writing skills, the more aware you become of other authors' techniques. The more you read – fiction, non-fiction, poetry, drama – the better your own writing will become. You absorb techniques, especially **rhythm**, at a subliminal or instinctive level.

Higher English Grade Booster will take you stage by stage through the specific skills needed for the entire English course and the Close Reading and the Critical Essay papers of the examination. It will also help prepare you for your personal study and the three internal assessments – your own piece of writing, the National Assessment Bank (NAB) Close Reading, and the NAB Textual Analysis.

Each chapter deals with a separate aspect of the course and the exam. You will find three elements in the book:

1. the techniques and skills you need;
2. worked examples of the application of the techniques; and
3. opportunities to practise applying the techniques yourself.

But first of all, let's look at all that is involved in the Higher coursework and examination:

THE COURSEWORK AND THE EXAMINATION

Higher English coursework comprises three units, all of which involve internal assessments, called unit assessments. The following table sets out the unit assessment requirements of Higher English:

Unit assessments

Unit number	Title	Internal assessment
Unit 1	Language Study	**Essay:** minimum of 650 words (pass / fail) + **Close reading:** 1 hour (pass / fail)
Unit 2	Literary Study	**Textual Analysis:** 45 minutes (pass / fail)
Unit 3	Personal Study	**Personal Study:** critical appreciation of a text of candidate's own choice, own topic completed under supervised conditions with the text available and own notes on 2 sides A4 (pass / fail)

Higher English Language Skills

All assessments are pass / fail – that is, they are not graded for Scottish Qualifications Authority (SQA).

The examination

There is also the external examination comprising two papers: Close Reading (worth 50 marks) and Critical Analysis (two essays, each worth 25 marks).

Paper	Questions
Close Reading (90 minutes)	Close Reading (Interpretation) – 2 linked passages, totalling 50 marks
Critical Analysis (90 minutes)	2 Critical Essays from more than one **genre**, each worth 25 marks = 50 marks

 Each of the unit assessments and the examination (as set out in the tables above) require knowledge of and skills in language. To study language you need tools, and the key aim of this book is to give you all those tools that you will require in every aspect of the Higher English course.

AN EXAMPLE OF ESSENTIAL KEY SKILLS: WORD ORDER

The first piece of work that you will probably tackle is the Personal Study. In consultation with your teacher, you must:

- choose your own text(s) from any genre;
- devise your own task;
- make notes of analysis and evaluation in line with the chosen task;
- write about 850 words on that task otherwise you may not pass (under supervised conditions) – though you are allowed to have with you the text and two A4 sides of notes.

Higher English Language Skills

This assessment is a perfect opportunity to practise and perfect the skills of critical analysis which are so essential in performing well in the Critical Essay paper in the examination in May.

To analyse effectively any text you need to have knowledge about language: you need to know about **narrative structure**, **paragraphs**, **sentence structure**, **linkage**, **punctuation**, **word choice** and the **connotations** of words. You need also to know about devices such as **metaphor**, **metonymy**, **alliteration** and **symbolism**.

Everything really has to do with meaning. Some people want to separate the *content* of a sentence from its *form* – that is, they want to distinguish between what the sentence says and the way that it says it. But that is rather an old-fashioned approach to analysis; in any case it is an approach that leads to confusion. It is not really possible to distinguish between a sentence and what it *says* or means.

 A sentence is what it says. You cannot separate content from form for one very important reason: whenever you change the form (the word order) of a sentence, you change the meaning.

It is vital to understand this aspect of sentence structure because some questions in both Textual Analysis and Close Reading can only be answered by recognising the relationship between sentence structure and meaning.

Let's take, for example, the sentence: *Only I saw Kevin.* We shall move the word *only* and note how each shift alters meaning:

Sentence	Meaning
Only I saw Kevin	Of all the people present (who were witnesses), I was the only one who saw Kevin
I only saw Kevin	That is, I didn't hear him
I saw only Kevin	There were many people present (to see), but the only one I saw was Kevin
I saw Kevin only	There was no-one else around but Kevin

You see how meaning is altered when you alter word order?

You must get to know about word order since the answers to many Close Reading (an entire paper worth 50 marks) and Textual Analysis (a NAB which you must pass) questions depend on that knowledge.

Higher English Language Skills

EXAM EXAMPLE

The following example is taken from an actual SQA Higher exam. In the Textual Analysis passage there was the sentence:

> *It was dark outside, and cold.*

The question was:

> **Comment on the effectiveness of the structure of this sentence.**

If you know about word order and meaning then you can easily answer that question:

> *because 'and cold' has been placed at the end of the sentence, therefore greater attention is drawn to its meaning, therefore the cold is being stressed.*

Let's look at another example from the 1996 Higher, Textual Analysis question. The text – a poem called *Waiting Room* by Moira Andrew – is about an old woman who is now living in a nursing home. When her family visit her, she finds it difficult to recall the names of other family members. The following lines appear:

> *Tormented,*
> *she tries to trap them on her tongue.*

This time the question was:

> **By close reference to language, comment on the effectiveness of these lines.**

And the answer could not be simpler –

> *the idea of torment is being stressed by placing the word 'Tormented' at the beginning of the sentence.*

Higher English **Grade Booster** 9

Remember that whenever we alter normal word order we alter meaning. (More will be said in detail about word order in chapter 5.) The answer to the above question also involves comment on the alliteration of the *t* and *tr* sounds and you may also note that in the above lines of poetry *Tormented* has been placed at the end of the line: these are both literary devices which also create emphasis. Both these devices – along with many others – will be discussed later. At the moment we are concentrating on word order.

This book will show you how to analyse structure and therefore understand meaning. It will also help you analyse effect by a close examination and analysis of the ways in which words are put together in a sentence – in other words, it will help you understand the grammar of the language. It will also, of course, show you how to put words together – grammatically – in the sentences that you yourself compose in your own writing!

WHAT IS GRAMMAR?

Grammar – or the ways in which words are put together in a sentence – is really the classification of common sense. To be absolutely accurate, grammar is the method of classifying the way in which language – any language – operates, whereas **syntax** is the way in which an individual sentence is put together, though the terms are often used interchangeably. Many individuals, especially nowadays, claim that they know no grammar, yet most of the time they speak and write perfectly grammatically. For example, as you will learn, there are three present tenses in English. It's possible, like most people, you didn't know that. Yet every native speaker of English uses the three present tenses without ever making a mistake. When someone asks you if you would like something to eat, you would never dream of replying: 'No thank you, I already eat'. You would say: 'I am already eating', employing, without thinking, the Continuous Present Tense. Of course, we all make grammatical mistakes sometimes since English is a complex language, but we make fewer grammatical mistakes than we realise.

The problem is that 'grammar' has a bad reputation. Even in the 1950s, 'grammar' was linked with the notion of correctness – only formal English was worth studying, and a knowledge of grammar was essential to enable you to speak and write 'correctly'. Since then, grammar has shifted towards the idea of *describing actual usage* and away from *prescribing 'correct' usage*. The teaching of grammar, however, was dropped from the English curriculum as a result of its reputation for correctness and difficulty, thus creating a generation of students and adults who do not have the grammatical tools to study language.

Higher English Language Skills

There are probably more than a million words in the English language. One of the reasons why English has such a huge vocabulary is because it is a very flexible, adaptable language and it loves **synonyms** – words which apparently have the same or similar meanings. For example, we have four words to describe a train which goes under the ground – *underground, metro, subway,* and *tube*. In French, on the other hand, there is only one word to describe such a train: *le metro*. English is adaptable: it will borrow words from other languages. The Newcastle *metro* is borrowed from French, and the Glasgow *subway* is from the Latin *sub* meaning 'below' and *via* meaning 'way' or 'route'. *Underground* is Anglo-Saxon and *tube* is clearly an image representing the tunnel-structure of underground railways.

The key aim of this book is to teach you a grammar that describes the way in which language is actually used. What you will learn is highly relevant to you at this point in your studies for Higher English. But it will do more than that: it will help you develop the skills to analyse and evaluate texts in all areas of assessment. You will enhance your language skills in ways that will enable you to gain the grade you want in the Higher.

When many candidates are faced with questions that ask them to comment on the effectiveness of the language of a given piece of text, they answer by giving the meaning. That is an inadequate response, but if you can answer by making an evaluative comment on effect then you are well on your way to an 'A' pass.

This book will help you develop your language skills: you will be better able to analyse language in whatever situation it is used and it will help you write grammatically-acceptable sentences and to punctuate accurately.

This book, then, is not just for Higher English but also for all time.

Higher English Language Skills

2 The Origins of English

What the Romans did for us
The introduction of English
The French influence
The re-emergence of English
The language of Shakespeare
The effect of trading
Summary

WHAT THE ROMANS DID FOR US

Two thousand years ago, these islands were sporadically populated by Celtic tribes. Those nearest the south coast of England must have been taken aback by the sudden and highly efficient invasion by the Romans. Very quickly, the Romans established their base in the south and east of what is now England and brought with them a civilising influence: roads, baths, central heating, sewerage systems, aqueducts, and the conquest of the Celts – though those Celts who have survived to the 21st century may not quite agree!

The Celts were not quite conquered. In the south, many – but not all – were probably kept as slaves, while others were displaced to the nethermost extremities of these islands, where they joined with the indigenous population in attacking Roman defences. Hadrian's Wall held back the northern marauding Celts, up to a point,

Higher English Grade Booster 13

but it is interesting that the border drawn by the Romans follows pretty much the same border between England and Scotland established over a millennium later, a fact which has probably more to do with lines of communication than bad Celtic behaviour! Although some Roman settlements existed as far north as the Forth-Clyde valley, nevertheless the long-term settlements and influences were in the south.

The Roman influence over the remaining indigenous population was much more cultural than it was military, affecting the Celts to the south both politically and, of course, linguistically: Latin became the dominant language.

The Romans themselves departed from these islands during the fifth century AD to deal with problems elsewhere in their empire, leaving behind people who spoke vulgar – or everyday – Latin and who had been much influenced by generations of Roman culture and control. The people of that southern area of these islands were known as Britons.

THE INTRODUCTION OF ENGLISH

With the departure of the Romans, the Scots and the Picts began consistently to invade the civilised south, to such an extent that the Britons sent for help from that north-western part of Europe (modern Germany and Denmark) which was then occupied by the Angles, Jutes and Saxons.

Though invited by the Britons to help protect them from the Scots and Picts, nevertheless the Angles, Jutes and Saxons soon took over the areas to the south and east of Britain, and with supreme arrogance referred to the native Britons as *wealas* ('foreigners') from which we get the modern word *Welsh*. Very soon the invaders themselves were referred to as Saxons (donating their name to those areas now called Middlesex, Essex, and Sussex).

Gradually, however, the term *Angli* began to have greater usage, and was used even by the Latin writers of the time (sixth century). The country began to be referred to as *Engla Land* and the language that the invaders had introduced as *Englisc* (pronounced 'English'). This is the period of the English language referred to as Anglo-Saxon or Old English.

THE FRENCH INFLUENCE

The relative stability did not last long: in 1065, there came another invasion, this time by William of Normandy (the Conqueror), who landed at Hastings and quickly established himself as monarch. He introduced not only the French language to the court but also greater centralisation, efficient administration, and effective organisation, all of which helped establish French as the dominant language. It quickly became the language of the ruling and upper classes, partly because William appointed French barons, French bishops, French court officials – in other words the whole upper crust of society. Even the French bourgeoisie crossed the Channel to exploit the new markets! For over 100 years French dominated the court, the parliament, all public proceedings and the law, though the language of the Church remained Latin; the lower classes, the peasants, however, continued to speak English.

THE RE-EMERGENCE OF ENGLISH

But during the 14th century, for a variety of reasons, English began to re-emerge as the language of the upper classes. We know this because the poet Geoffrey Chaucer, very much involved at court, chose to write his *Canterbury Tales* in English, a decision that would have made no sense if the dominant language had still been French. Nevertheless, the English that he used demonstrates the French influence on the language, an influence which exists to this day.

Look at the following extract from the very beginning of The Prologue to *The Canterbury Tales*. Although written more than 600 years ago, much of it is still recognisable:

> *Whan that Aprille with his shoures soote*
> *The droghte of March hath perced to the roote*
> *And bathed every veyne in swich licour,*
> *Of which vertu engendred is the flour...*

You get the idea that the sweet April showers pierce to the root the droughts of March and thus create such liquid that flowers begin to grow. You recognise words such as 'shoures', 'droghte', 'bathed', 'licour' and 'flour'; indeed, 'soote' is probably the only word that you couldn't translate, though you could guess at its meaning.

The changes that take place in the language over the next 200 years inevitably bring the language closer to the one that we all recognise, though it is still obviously not Modern English. The pace of change was much slower in the 15th and 16th centuries, mainly because the language was almost entirely spoken and only written and read by that rare breed, the highly educated. There were no newspapers, television, film, radio, aeroplanes, mobile phones, CDs, DVDs, iPods, the Internet – communication was limited, mostly geographically, to the few people that any individual would have known. In contrast, changes to the language increased exponentially throughout the 20th century and in this century the pace will be even more rapid, thanks mainly to continuing technological development.

However, some 530 years ago, in the late 1470s, there was a huge technological development that had a revolutionary effect on the language: the printing press was introduced into this country by William Caxton. The consequences of that invention on linguistic, literary, social, and educational development were enormous. Prior to its invention, all books had to be produced by hand, a labour of love that must have been more enriching to the scribe than it would have been effective: so few books were produced by such a labour intensive method that there would have been no need to teach people to read and write, unless, of course, they were going to become a scribe or a translator. Once, however, the printing press came to this land many more books could be produced and it must have added gigabytes to the collective memory. Libraries and bookshops became possible, and increasing numbers of people had to learn to read and write. Schools began to flourish and language began to develop in the written mode.

THE LANGUAGE OF SHAKESPEARE

Geoffrey Chaucer, who wrote *The Canterbury Tales*, died in 1400. William Shakespeare began writing nearly 200 years later, when Elizabeth I was still in her glorious reign. Produced below is an extract from one of his plays, *As You Like It*, written in 1599. Clearly, the language is now much closer to our own than it is to the language used by Chaucer. The spelling and the sentence structure are much more recognisable, and no doubt you will agree that even some of the vocabulary is very familiar! One of the characters in the play – Jacques – reflects on the nature of human existence. He says that all the world is a stage and that in life we play many parts, but they can be categorised into seven acts. Here are the first two acts:

> At first the infant,
> Mewling and puking in the nurse's arms;
> Then, the whining schoolboy with his satchel
> And shining morning face, creeping like snail
> Unwillingly to school…

The language may have changed somewhat over 400 years, but babies still behave in the same way and schoolboy sentiments haven't altered one whit!

THE EFFECT OF TRADING

Another major effect on our language occurred during the 18th century when many trading and seafaring terms entered the language from other European countries, especially as trade developed with north-west Europe and the Netherlands. In the 19th century and early 20th century, Britain established and developed its Empire, bringing to these shores a quantity and variety of vocabulary that not only enriched our language but has had a lasting effect on it, again showing the extent to which English can absorb vocabulary in a way in which few other languages can. But of course, trading and particularly emigration meant that the language was spread to Canada, the USA, and Australasia, which in turn reinvigorated English in their own ways.

SUMMARY

This chapter has put into historical context the development of the English language and has shown that the influences on the language that we speak and write date from the first millennium:

- the indigenous Celtic language almost replaced by Latin, though less so in the north and west;
- the influx of Angles, Jutes, and Saxons who brought with them their language that eventually became Old English, though the influences of Celtic and especially Latin were considerable and much Latin vocabulary was retained;
- the invasion in 1066 by the Normans who brought with them words to do with political organisation – *government, parliament, centralisation, authority* – and were responsible for the eventual supremacy of the French language among the upper classes; for a time French became the dominant language but it was eventually replaced by English, which, once more, retained the influence of the language it was replacing;
- the eventual emergence of English as the language most widely used in this country – considerably influenced by Celtic, Latin, and French;
- the effects of trading, especially with Europe, and the growth of the British Empire brought many vocabulary items to English – and, of course, helped spread English to all parts of the world, especially throughout North America and Australasia.

2 The Origins of English

Because the English language has been exposed to so many influences over the last 1200–1400 years, it is one of the most flexible languages in the world and will absorb words from all cultures readily and easily. In the 1960s, with the emergence of space travel, the language was comfortable with the word *astronaut* (Greek) or the word *cosmonaut* (Russian with Greek derivation) or, quite simply *spaceman* (French + Old English). Consequently, with its ability to use so many synonyms, English has developed an enormous vocabulary.

This chapter has not only given you an idea of the historical context of the language you speak and write, but has also given you an idea of the various languages embedded in English. **Tone** in English often has to do with the origin of the vocabulary item that you employ: thus words of French origin tend to be more diplomatic and political in tone, whereas Anglo-Saxon words are much more related to everyday things and to our most powerful emotions. Latinate words tend to be more philosophical and reflective in tone. We will look more closely at tone in chapter 12.

3   What is Grammar?

Why bother with grammar?
The basics
Analysing texts
Levels of analysis
Examples for you to try

WHY BOTHER WITH GRAMMAR?

There are three main reasons why grammar is important – and each has relevance to the Higher:

1. since the main purpose of language is to express thoughts and feelings – to communicate – the more precisely we can use language the more effectively we will communicate;
2. a knowledge of grammar will mean that your ability to express yourself accurately and clearly in your own writing will be greatly increased;
3. a knowledge of grammar will mean higher marks throughout much of the course and particularly in the Close Reading paper.

There is also a fourth reason. By understanding the grammar of our language we not only gain an insight into the way the language works but we can also appreciate greater subtleties and shades of meaning.

THE BASICS

First of all you need some basic knowledge. You are already aware from the Introduction that the order in which words appear in a sentence determines the

3 What is Grammar?

meaning. But it's a bit more complicated than that: not only does word order determine meaning, but there are rules which govern the way we put sentences together. For example, we can say:

> *The boy ate the banana outside the school gates*

and we can even say

> *Outside the school gates, the boy ate the banana*

though it means something slightly different – the second example draws attention to where the boy ate the banana rather than that he ate it.

We cannot, however, say:

> *Outside the boy ate the banana school gates the*

simply because the sentence is meaningless. We have broken the rules – or grammar – of the sentence to such an extent that it no longer makes sense.

Grammar and meaning are therefore linked, and the greater our knowledge of grammar the more we will understand meaning and, therefore, the better able we will be to make meaning clear – especially in the written mode. The study of grammar gives you a clearer understanding of the way in which language works.

ANALYSING TEXTS

To be able to analyse a text properly you need to be able to comment on **sentence structure**, **tense**, and the effect of certain kinds of words such as **adverbs**, **adjectives**, and **present participles**. This is particularly true of Close Reading, where some of the questions, especially those specifically about sentence structure, require a knowledge of grammar to answer them effectively.

In order to achieve a good grade in the Higher, you need to understand the various stages of grammatical analysis such that you will be able to recognise and analyse **sentences**, **clauses**, **groups**, and **individual words**. Moreover you need to learn about punctuation and its role in the clarification of meaning. You also need to master the rules of spelling, and further in this book we offer you some guidelines to make this easier.

What is Grammar?

At this point we need to stress a general, but very important, point about grammar: in the earlier part of the 20th century 'rules' of grammar were taught in schools, and these rules were very largely based on Latin grammar, laying down how English *ought* to be written or spoken. In a sense, English was made to fit the very precise rules of Latin. By the middle of the century, however, there was a change in thinking about grammar, and the linguists of the time realised that grammar should not be 'prescriptive', dictating the rules for correct usage, but should be 'descriptive'; that is, the grammar should describe how the English language is actually used and *not* how it ought to be used.

This book takes its cue from the modern school of thought and sets out the grammar that describes usage. But that can create a problem: English is changing constantly – today we speak and spell and write and punctuate English in ways quite differently from those who were alive in the 18th century – and there are purists who may well regret some of these changes. This book sets out to describe the way in which we actually use English today while at the same time informing you about what some people still see as the 'correct' form of the language.

 One more thing. Let's again make the distinction between 'grammar' and 'syntax' quite clear: 'grammar' is the word we use to describe the entire system by which we classify the language and the way in which it works, whereas 'syntax' is the word we use for the way in which a single sentence is put together. Syntax is, then, a subset of grammar.

LEVELS OF ANALYSIS

There are four main levels of analysis: **sentence**, **clause**, **group**, **word**:

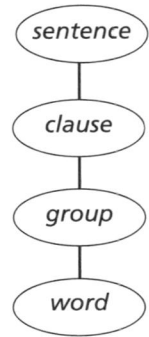

There is, then, a kind of natural progression of analysis. We can start by examining the sentence:

1. analyse the sentence and break it down into its clauses; then
2. analyse the clauses and break them down into groups; then
3. analyse the groups by examining and labelling the words; then
4. analyse the words by examining how the word has been made up.

In this book, however, we will examine words themselves before we examine word groups, since you need to know about *verbs*, *nouns* and *adjectives* before you can discuss word groups (see chapter 5).

Words can also be analysed in terms of their constituent syllables: thus, the word 'sentence' is made up of two syllables – sen / tence.

Sentences

A **sentence** is a word or a combination of words which makes complete sense. It does not have to contain a verb. Thus ***No!*** is a sentence as well as the following sentence from *Marrakech* by George Orwell:

> Not hostile, not contemptuous, not sullen, not even inquisitive.

Again, Orwell's sentence does not contain a verb – i.e. it is a verbless or **minor sentence**.

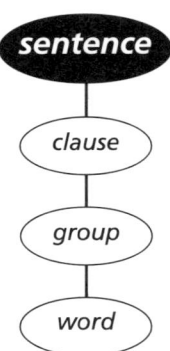

There are four kinds of sentences:

1. The Statement: *The cow jumped over the moon.*
2. The Interrogative: *Did the cow jump over moon?*
   (or question)
3. The Imperative: *Jump over the moon!*
   (or command)
4. The Interjection: *Alas!*

Clauses

A clause is a group of words containing one main **verb**. If the group of words can stand alone and make sense then the clause is a **main clause**. A sentence contains at least one main clause. Take, for example, the sentence:

> *Thomas ate the apple.*

Clearly, since there is only one clause (there is only one main verb – 'ate') and since the clause stands alone making sense this is a main clause. In the sentence:

> *Thomas ate the apple when he left the shop.*

there are two clauses because there are two main verbs – 'Thomas *ate* the apple' and 'when he *left* the shop'. This second clause cannot stand alone and make sense, therefore it is known as a **subordinate clause** (or **dependent clause**) because it is subordinate to the main clause – it depends on the main clause in order for it to make sense.

EXAMPLES FOR YOU TO TRY

Now you try to work out which are the main and which are the subordinate clauses in the following sentences:

1. Mary had a little lamb.
2. I saw a ship on the horizon.
3. As the train slowed, I gathered together all my luggage.
4. English is my favourite subject because it is so fascinating.
5. I wandered lonely as a cloud that floats on high o'er vales and hills. (Wordsworth)

4 Subordinate Clauses

Subordination – worked example
Minor sentences
Exam example
Examples for you to try

```
sentence
  |
clause
  |
group
  |
word
```

Although the last chapter may seem complicated, it isn't – it is only unfamiliar. The terms *main clause* and *subordinate clause* can allow you to talk more easily about sentences.

Very often, in Close Reading, you are asked to comment on the **style** of a passage. For example, here is one question recently asked in Close Reading (Question on Both Passages section):

> Which passage did you find more stimulating? In your answer you should refer to the style of both passages.

If you know about subordinate clauses, the question becomes easier to answer.

SUBORDINATION – WORKED EXAMPLE

In formal writing, you come across a great deal of subordination – i.e. there are more **subordinate clauses** than usual:

Look at the following paragraph from *The Girl in Winter* by Philip Larkin.

> There had been no more snow during the night, but **because** the frost continued so that the drifts lay **where** they had fallen, people told each other there was more to come. **When** it grew lighter, it seemed that they were right, **for** there was no sun, only one vast shell of cloud over the fields and woods. In contrast to the snow the sky looked brown. Indeed, without the snow the

24 *Higher English* **Grade Booster**

Subordinate Clauses 4

morning would have resembled a January nightfall, **for** *what light there was seemed to rise up from it.*

Now you can see the number of clauses beginning with *because, where, when, for* – in other words there are many subordinate clauses, a marker of formal prose. Another feature of formal prose is the placing of a subordinate clause at the beginning of a sentence. Look at the third line of the above paragraph, the sentence beginning on that line:

When it grew lighter, *it seemed that they were right, for there was no sun, only one vast shell of cloud over the fields and woods.*

The main clause in this sentence is *it seemed that they were right*, but note that the subordinate clause *When it grew lighter* comes at the beginning of the sentence – a feature of formal prose.

MINOR SENTENCES

A feature of informal prose is the **minor sentence** – a sentence without a verb. Look at the following passage:

Dead romantic, eh? Forget it. Sad, is what it is. Sad and scary. You're leaving a place you know and heading into the unknown with nothing to protect you. No money. No prospect of work. No address where folks will make you welcome.

Look at the number of minor sentences in the above extract from *Stone Cold* by Robert Swindells. Their use is a marker of informal prose, and in this case the effect is to create in writing the rhythms of spoken English.

 When you are asked to comment on the effectiveness of style in the Close Reading paper, you now know that one aspect of style is the type of sentences being used: if there is subordination – the presence of many subordinate clauses and/or subordinate clauses at the beginning of sentences – then the style is formal. If, on the other hand, there are minor sentences the style is informal, even colloquial. Equally, when you are writing formally – as you ought to be doing in the Critical Essay paper – you, too, must remember to use subordinate clauses to give your writing formality and style.

Higher English **Grade Booster** 25

4 Subordinate Clauses

EXAM EXAMPLE

Let's look at an example from a passage used in an SQA past paper.

> *As it was, malnourished, in rags, gnawed at daily by corrupting influences, discouraged everywhere, and perpetually tired through sleeping in a room with his brother and sister, where his mother and her horrible paramour also slept, he could still hold his own among the cleverest of his contemporaries.*

Here the main clause is *he could still hold his own among the cleverest of his contemporaries* and there are several subordinate clauses coming before that main clause. If you were asked to comment on the style of the passage, you would refer to this sentence, point out that the subordinate clauses come before the main clause and that therefore the style is formal.

EXAMPLES FOR YOU TO TRY

Is the style of the following sentences formal or informal? In your answer you should refer to the position of the subordinate clauses:

1. When he replied quietly, with no shame or even shyness, that he had never really seen the sea, they sneered at him.

2. Although he had read the question paper for fifteen minutes, he still could not answer any of the questions.

3. Good isn't it? Couldn't believe my eyes. It's a great wee car, isn't it?

4. Yet when I look at my children as they lie sleeping, arms flung above their heads, a puff of breath fluttering on their upper lip, I see by their rapid eye movement that they must be asleep.

Now of course there are other markers of formality/informality, but one of the easiest ways to identify formal prose is to examine the position of the subordinate clauses. And you should remember that in your own writing.

26 *Higher English* **Grade Booster**

5 Analysing the Words

Word classes

Worked example 1

Word groups – pre- and post-modification

Worked example 2 – pre-modification

Worked example 3 – post-modification

Examples for you to try

Word groups – propositional phrases

Worked example 4

Exam example

Examples for you to try

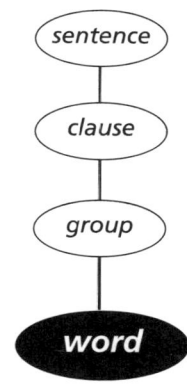

Before we examine word groups, we need to recognise the various **word classes**. This is a process that used to be called **parsing** – identifying the parts of speech by means of their function.

WORD CLASSES

In order to classify words, we refer to eight **parts of speech**:

1. **Noun**
2. **Pronoun**
3. **Adjective**
4. **Verb**
5. **Adverb**
6. **Preposition**
7. **Conjunction**
8. **Interjection**

but, of course, these subdivide further. It is really important to recognise that we cannot classify a word in isolation from its context, that is, isolated from the

Higher English **Grade Booster** 27

5 Analysing the Words

sentence in which it is being used. An example will make this clearer for you: the word 'table' is clearly a noun, you might say. But what is it in the sentence 'I want to table the motion that all grammar is really quite exciting'? Clearly, *in that context*, the word 'table' is a verb.

WORKED EXAMPLE 1

In the poem *Pike* by Ted Hughes the first verse opens with the following lines:

> *Pike, three inches long, perfect*
> *Pike in all parts, green tigering the gold.*

You can recognise that the word *tigering* has been **coined** by Hughes and that in this context it is clearly a verb, and as such draws attention to its meaning: that the fish are tiger-like in that they have stripes (like tigers), they are predators, and they are ferociously vicious.

 Note that I have made four points: I have recognised the language feature (the noun used as a verb) and I have made three comments on its effect.

He also describes the aquarium in which he kept pike:

> *Three we kept behind glass,*
> *Jungled in weed:*

Here, Hughes has once again coined the word *jungled*, making a verb of a noun. If you know and understand the terms *noun* and *verb* any question about these coined words becomes so much easier to answer.

A question very likely to be asked about the lines from Ted Hughes' *Pike* might be:

> **By close reference to any language feature, show how effectively Hughes creates the image of pike.** [2 marks]

Now you know how to answer! There are two marks available, therefore you should try to make two points. Your answer would be:

28 *Higher English* Grade Booster

Analysing the Words

> *In his use of 'jungled', Ted Hughes has taken a noun and turned it into a verb* [1 mark]
> *thereby associating the image of the pike with brutal, predatory animals and the dangers of the jungle.* [1 mark]

See how easy it becomes? And all because you can recognise that a noun has been used as a verb.

Interestingly, the North Americans are fond of converting nouns to verbs – e.g. *to goal, to trial*. Maybe the next one will be *to verb*!

It is, however, important that you are able to recognise all word classes. In order to make it easier for you to learn, recognise, and understand the functions of words, the table below classifies words for you.

Word Classes

Word Class	Function	Example
(1) **NOUN**	Usually defined as the name of something, though some words which may look like nouns can be, within a given context, a verb. American English readily uses nouns as verbs – e.g. *to goal (as in score a goal), she just texted (as in sent a text)*	*Boy, girl, man, dog, couch, vegetables, fish, meat, ironmongers, calculator, channel, television*
Concrete noun	The name of something which actually exists and can be seen, heard, touched, etc.	*Lion, human, pen, star, chair, moon, sun, nose, ear*
Abstract noun	The name of an emotion or feeling – something that you cannot touch. Often these words end in *–ness*.	*Happiness, sadness, tiredness, grief, excitement, hearing, eyesight, loveliness, beauty, nosiness, cleanliness, uprightness, merriment, backwardness, intelligence, boredom, freedom, martyrdom, kingdom, earldom*

Higher English **Grade Booster** 29

5 Analysing the Words

Word Classes

Word Class	Function	Example
Proper noun	A person's name; the name of a town, country, city. Please remember that Proper nouns must begin with a capital letter!	*Aberdeen, Dundee, Fife, Scotland, Darren, Fiona, Buster*
Collective noun	The name given to a group of animals or objects	*A **pack** of wolves, a **flock** of sheep, a **herd** of cows, a **bunch** of flowers, a **pride** of lions, a **gaggle** of geese*
(2) PRONOUN	A word which stand for a noun	*He, she, we, you, they, them, his, hers, theirs, our, ours, yours, mine, it, its, your, myself, yourself, him / herself, themselves*
Relative pronoun	Used after a noun to avoid repeating the noun – *who, whom, whose, which, that, as*	*That is the man **who** crossed the road; this is the woman **whose** house has just been sold; this is the snake **which** escaped from the zoo; I have marked the wall **that** has just been painted; such men **as** these make good teachers*
(3) ADJECTIVE	A word which describes things or people – adjectives, then, modify meaning	*Beautiful, pretty, excited, tired, happy, sad, clever, intelligent, bored*
Compound adjective	A word made up of two words to describe some thing or person	*Long-blind, hunchback-born, half-paralysed*
Comparative and superlative adjectives	Where you have the absolute adjective (e.g. *thin*), the comparative (*thinner*) and the superlative (*thinnest*)	*Good, better, best* *Bad, worse, worst* *Happy, happier, happiest* (or *Happy, more happy, most happy*)

Analysing the Words

Word Classes

Word Class	Function	Example
Demonstrative adjectives	Sometimes known as a determiner – usually refers to an antecedent. Can also be a pronoun. Words such as – *this* (referring to something near the speaker), *that* (referring to something distant), *these, those*	*This* coat is nicer than *that* one over there. All *this* goes to show...
Definite article (has an adjectival function)	The word *the* modifies (alters) the meaning of a noun. Note the difference between *man* and *the man*	*The* lion, *the* boy, *the* car, *the* bus, *the* new livery
Indefinite article (has an adjectival function)	The words *a* and *an*	*An* apple, *a* flock of sheep, *a* gaggle of schoolboys, *a* collection of books, *an* extraordinary adventure
(4) **VERB**	Difficult to define, though the traditional definition is the *doing word*. Sometimes verbs do not *do*, however, such as the verb *to be*. The infinitive is preceded by *to*.	*To skip, to run, to jump, to think, to reflect, to predict, to speak, to write, to spell, to understand, to read, to play, to look, to cross, to hear, to touch*
The –ing participle (traditionally known as the present participle)	The *–ing* word when it is part of the verb: normally, but not always, part of the present tense! We also use *–ing* participles with the past continuous tense – see the example opposite. Hence, it is inaccurate to refer to it as a *present* participle.	*I am running, walking, jumping* but also: *I was running, I was choking*

Higher English **Grade Booster** 31

5 Analysing the Words

Word Classes

Word Class	Function	Example
Other words ending in –ing (traditionally known as a gerund)	Where the word ending in –ing is said to act more as a noun, but the problem is that it isn't quite a noun and still has a verb-like function.	*A pedestrian crossing, a walking stick*
The past participle	The way we form the past tense: we add –ed to the end of the root verb, though this is not the only way to form the past tense!	*We have walked, I have jumped, he has played*
(5) **ADVERB**	A word which modifies or alters the meaning of the verb – in English the adverb frequently ends in –ly and usually answer questions such as *why, when, how*. But watch out for words such as *then, however, moreover* – which are also adverbs.	*Beautifully, lovely, playfully, excitedly, merrily, happily, sadly, tiredly, slowly, bluntly, however, furthermore*
(6) **PREPOSITIONS**	Words which indicate relationships between objects	*On, under, below, on top, beside, beneath, above, through, into, at, in*
Prepositional phrase	A phrase which begins with a preposition – often at the beginning of a sentence	*In the morning, on the sink, on the table, at the pictures, in the English classroom, in France, on the sea, under the bed, beside the coffee table*
(7) **CONJUNCTIONS**	Linking or joining words, but please note that *however* is not a conjunction – it is an adverb	*And, because, but, or, since*
(8) **INTERJECTION**	Sounds which are inserted into a sentence to attract the attention of the person addressed or to express emotion. Interjections have a dramatic effect.	*Hark! Hush! Alas! Bravo! But try not to use the double exclamation mark, which looks unstylish.*

WORD GROUPS – PRE- AND POST-MODIFICATION

Now that you know how to classify words, we can take a closer look at groups of words, sometimes referred to as phrases. (A **phrase** is a group of words which does not contain a **verb** – see the table on page 31.) We can now look at the function of a group of words within the context of a sentence. It's easier to explain using an example.

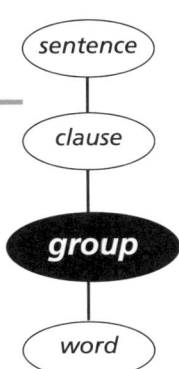

WORKED EXAMPLE 2 – PRE-MODIFICATION

Look at the following sentence:

The 44-year old, tall, blonde, Surbiton housewife refused to speak to our reporter.

Let's examine the word group – the group coming before the verb (in this case *refused*) and sometimes referred to as the **nominal group**:

The 44-year old, tall, blonde, Surbiton housewife

Now, which is the most important word, or headword, in this group? Clearly, it is the **noun** *housewife*. (You should keep referring to the table on pages 29–32 for word classifications.) The other words in the group are all **adjectives**. (Although we classify the word *the* as a **definite article**, nevertheless it has the function of an **adjective**.) Next, note the position of the adjectives – they all come before the main word, and that is another feature of informal prose style. Tabloid newspapers invariably place all the adjectives before the main noun that they are describing. Since these adjectives describe – or modify – the main word and because they come before it their function is called **pre-modification**.

As mentioned above, the word *the*, though a **definite article**, nevertheless performs the function of an **adjective** in that it is modifying the meaning of the main noun. To clarify further: there is a difference in meaning between *The 44-year old, tall, blonde, Surbiton housewife* (a particular housewife is being referred to) and *A 44-year old, tall, blonde, Surbiton housewife* (a Surbiton housewife randomly selected) or even *One 44-year old, tall, blonde, Surbiton housewife* (one out of several possible Surbiton housewives). Hence the definite and **indefinite articles** (and numbers) have an adjectival function.

WORKED EXAMPLE 3 – POST-MODIFICATION

Let's look at the following sentence:

Brad Pitt, the world famous movie star, was interviewed on television last night.

Let's examine the word group:

Brad Pitt, the world famous movie star

This time, the most important word, or headword, is the proper noun *Brad Pitt*. But although there are no adjectives preceding *Brad Pitt*, there is a phrase following it: *the world famous movie star,* a phrase which acts like – or has the same function as – an adjective. This time, though, the phrase is coming after the main word, therefore we refer to it as **post-modification**. Such post-modification is a feature of more formal English that we would associate, say, with a broadsheet – or quality – newspaper.

A point of information: because *Brad Pitt* and the *world famous movie star* are the same person and refer to the same thing, the second phrase – *the world famous movie star* – is said to be in **apposition**. For example, in the sentence:

Tony Blair, Britain's Prime Minister, told our political editor, Andrew Marr, that he would fight crime and the causes of crime.

the phrase *Britain's Prime Minister* is in apposition to *Tony Blair* and *Andrew Marr* is in apposition to *our political editor*. You do not really need to know the term **apposition** (though to be able to use it shows that you are well-educated), therefore we will continue to refer to that word group as **post-modification**.

Of course we can change the word order by placing the modification in front of the main word *Brad Pitt*.

World famous movie star, Brad Pitt

You will recognise the style as that of a tabloid newspaper, where modification frequently comes before the main word to give the text a more racy, up-beat feel. Note also the lack of the word *the* before *world famous* – another feature of informal English.

Analysing the Words 5

EXAMPLES FOR YOU TO TRY

The following are extracts taken from newspapers: people's names have been altered to avoid embarrassment.

By a close examination of the language of the following sentences, comment on the structure of the following sentences:

1. Anguished Coronation Street actress, Deborah Winterbottom, said she was devastated to be written out of the show.

2. A shock *People* investigation reveals that top-class Rangers star, Freddie Sweet, had his car vandalised by disgruntled fans.

3. Dame Alison Campbell, one of Britain's most famous Shakespearean actresses, broke down in tears last night during the final scene of *The Taming of the Shrew*.

4. Vicious, ten year old, clueless tabby cat, suspiciously named Earl Grey, was removed by vets after biting its owner.

WORD GROUPS – PREPOSITIONAL PHRASES

A **prepositional phrase** is just what it says: a phrase beginning with a preposition. Let's take the sentence:

> *John drove down the motorway in the morning.*

Now, in this sentence there are two prepositional phrases: *down the motorway* and *in the morning*.

Look at this next sentence:

> *Alison went to the library with her overdue book under her arm.*

Again, there are two prepositional phrases: *to the library* and *with her overdue book*.

WORKED EXAMPLE 4

The point about prepositional phrases is that they follow a natural or obvious word order. If you change that word order by placing the prepositional phrase in another part of the sentence you then change the meaning. Take the first example above. Let's shift the prepositional phrase *in the morning* to the beginning of the sentence:

> *In the morning, John drove down the motorway.*

Now, by placing the phrase at the beginning of the sentence we draw attention to it, stressing not *that* John drove down the motorway but *when* he drove down the motorway.

In the second example, let's once more shift one of the prepositional phrases to the beginning of the sentence:

> *With her overdue book under her arm, Alison went to the library.*

Again we alter the meaning, this time drawing attention to the overdue book and the way in which Alison is carrying it – a purposeful, suggestion of defiance?

EXAM EXAMPLE

Now let's look at a more complex example, taken from an SQA past paper. This sentence appeared in an extract from Charles Dickens' novel *Our Mutual Friend*:

> *As they glided slowly on, keeping under the shore, and sneaking in and out among the shipping, by back-alleys of water, in a pilfering way that seemed to be their boatman's normal manner of progression, all the objects among which they crept were so huge in contrast with their wretched boat as to threaten to crush it.*

The question was:

> **Explain how the structure of the (above) sentence of this passage reflects the idea of the phrase 'in a pilfering way' (second line).**

First, you need to have an idea of what *in a pilfering way* means – *to pilfer* is to steal minor items, but here it is used about the way in which the boat moves stealthily, like a sneak-thief, in and out of larger ships. Now look how the sheer number of prepositional phrases supports that idea of moving in and out:

> *As they glided slowly on, under the shore, sneaking in and out, among the shipping, by back-alleys of water, and in a pilfering way.*

These phrases capture the idea of movement in and out and around, thus creating and supporting the image of the furtiveness of the boat's movement.

Analysing the Words

EXAMPLES FOR YOU TO TRY

Alter the position of the prepositional phrases in the following sentences and comment on the consequent effect on meaning:

1. There is an unbelievably dangerous sweep of the river between these two islands.

2. With Mobile 50+, it's easier to keep in touch.

3. Yesterday, in the championships, I won the race.

4. Along the canal bank, about twenty metres from the towpath, just beneath the hawthorn hedge bordering the field, I saw the body.

It is worth noting at this point that when you shift the prepositional phrase from the normal word order, you really should insert a comma after the phrase – as in examples 2, 3, and 4 above.

6 Sentence Structure

Worked example 1

Exam example

Worked example 2

An example for you to try

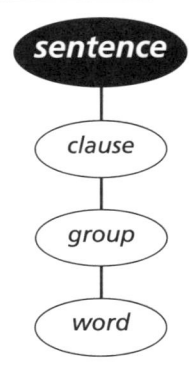

sentence — clause — group — word

In any language assessment paper, especially in Higher English Close Reading and the Textual Analysis assessment, there will be questions about sentence structure. We have already examined **pre-** and **post-modification,** and we have studied **prepositional phrases,** all of which means we know something about sentence structure – at least we know that shifting or altering the position of a phrase will alter meaning.

Invariably, there will be a question about sentence structure. Sometimes the question is in the format:

> **By referring to sentence structure, show how the writer conveys tone**

or in the format

> **Show how the writer uses sentence structure to demonstrate his/her strength of feeling in lines xx-yy.**

Too many candidates have difficulty in answering such questions about sentence structure, but by the end of this chapter you will have no difficulty whatsoever *because* you now know some grammar.

Sentence Structure

> Grammar is a useful, if not an essential, tool in the analysis of sentence structure.

WORKED EXAMPLE 1

Here are three lines from *Waiting Room* by Moira Andrew. Let's use the knowledge we now have to analyse the lines grammatically – or linguistically:

> *With the top of her mind*
> *She is eager to skim off news*
> *of the family*

Instantly, we note that the prepositional phrase *With the top of her mind* is at the beginning of the sentence – please remember that we are looking purely at the language of the poem and not the imagery or poetic aspects of it. By placing the prepositional phrase *With the top of her mind* right at the beginning of the sentence the poet has drawn the reader's attention to it, thus we become aware of the importance to the woman of the news of her family – it is foremost in her mind.

> It is by the analysis of the sentence structure that we are best able to comment on the effectiveness of the sentence.

EXAM EXAMPLE

The following, used in an SQA past paper, is from an extract concerning the exploits of Cortez as he conquered Mexico for the Spanish. This sentence concludes the extract:

> *Canal by canal, garden by garden, home by home, he destroyed what he had described to Charles V as 'the most beautiful city in the world'.*

The question was asked:

> **Comment fully on the effectiveness of the sentence structure as a conclusion to the passage.** [4 marks]

Higher English **Grade Booster** 39

6. Sentence Structure

> The number of marks attached to a question is a clear guide to the answer: in this case, with 4 marks allocated, you should try to make at least 4 points – 2 points which identify structural features and 2 points commenting on their effectiveness or, put another way, 2 marks for analysis and 2 marks for evaluation.

Look at the word groups:

> *Canal by canal, garden by garden, home by home, he destroyed what he had described to Charles V as 'the most beautiful city in the world'.*

We can make four points about the structure:

- **Alteration of normal word order**

    Right away we notice that the normal word order has been altered, and the word groups (phrases) have been placed at the beginning of the sentence – *Canal by canal, garden by garden, home by home* – thus drawing attention to them and thereby stressing their meaning: Cortez destroyed these things deliberately and methodically.

- **List**

    These items – *Canal by canal, garden by garden, home by home* – are in the form of a list, and if you look closely at the list you see that it begins with the impersonal (canals) and gets increasingly personal (homes). The list, then, is also in climactic structure – building up from canals to the destruction of individual homes – thus further drawing attention to the calculated, viciously cruel demolition of the city.

- **Repetition (parallel structure)**

    But also notice the **repetition** of the structure in the phrases *canal by canal, garden by garden,* and *home by home*: the formula is '*x* by *x*' and is repeated. If you look closely at each item you see that there is a repetition of the structure of each phrase as in the repetition of a formula – and the formula is '*x* by *x*' (repeated). Such repetition of phrases (of which this is a good example) is called *parallel structure*, the effect of which is always emphatic, thus enhancing meaning by drawing attention to it. The 'he' who is doing the destroying is doing it 'canal by canal', 'garden by garden', and 'home by home'. In other words the very structure of the sentence – the alteration of the normal word order, the listing of the phrases, and the parallel structure – powerfully suggests that the destruction was systematic, determined and ruthless.

- **Climactic structure**

    The use of the list, the parallel structure, the piling up of the word groups, the delay of the main point to the end of the sentence all combine to create a powerful **climax** or **climactic structure**, making the sentence highly dramatic. There are, then, two points that can be made about climax: the list moves climactically from the impersonal to the personal *and* the main point – the destruction of the most beautiful city in the world – is delayed to the very end.

WORKED EXAMPLE 2

Here is another example, this time a couple of sentences from a piece in which Robert Louis Stevenson reflects on Edinburgh's weather:

> *She is liable to be beaten upon by all the winds that blow, to be drenched with rain, to be buried in cold sea fogs out of the east, and powdered with the snow as it comes flying southward from the Highland hills. The weather is raw and boisterous in winter, shifty and ungenial in summer, and downright meteorological purgatory in the spring.*

Take the first sentence:

> *She is liable to be beaten upon by all the winds that blow, to be drenched with rain, to be buried in cold sea fogs out of the east, and powdered with the snow as it comes flying southward from the Highland hills.*

This time the word order is normal, but the word groups – *to be beaten upon by all the winds that blow, to be drenched with rain, to be buried in cold sea fogs out of the east, and powdered with the snow as it comes flying southward from the Highland hills* – are in the form of a **list**, and each item is also in **parallel structure**, this time in a 'to be *x*' formula. Again, the items in the list (each longer than in the previous example) are all built up in **climactic structure**. The total effect of all these **linguistic devices** is to reinforce the idea that the weather in Edinburgh is appallingly dismal!

6 Sentence Structure

AN EXAMPLE FOR YOU TO TRY

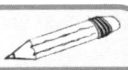

The following extract is from a past SQA paper:

> ...we have lost sight of the real purposes of education, namely to enable people to realise their own potential, develop their rational qualities and have the means and the chance to shape and change their own lives for their good and for the general good of society.
>
> And while I agree that one's opportunity to achieve these things is severely restricted if one has little money, having a paid job does not necessarily bring them out. Having a job is important but by making education serve that end we have failed people. Instead of holding fast to a vision of what really matters – our relationships with others, the quality of our friendships, our ability to be good parents, freedom to think for ourselves and to make choices, beauty, creativity, adventure, a sense of self worth – we have lowered our sights and reduced education to an assembly line through which we process children with the ultimate goal of passing exams.

The question asked that year was:

> **Show how the final sentence provides an effective conclusion to the passage. In your answer you should refer to such language features as: word choice, sentence structure, tone, punctuation...** [3 marks]

We will be dealing with word choice, tone, and punctuation in later chapters, but we can answer the question on sentence structure alone. Don't worry about trying to show how they provide an effective conclusion – again we will examine how to answer that kind of question later – but what I would like you to do is identify features of sentence structure and comment on their effectiveness [1 mark for the feature and 2 marks for the comment].

7 Further Features of Sentence Structure

Exam examples 1–2
Rhetoric
Something for you to try
Exam examples 3–4
Examples for you to try
Another example for you to try

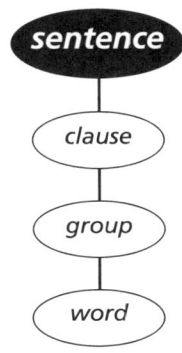

sentence — clause — group — word

You now know about certain aspects of sentence structure such as: the alteration of word order, the use of lists, and the use of parallel structure. You know in general terms the effects of these linguistic devices. Now we need to examine some of these devices more closely and have a look at some other features of sentence structure.

Questions about sentence structure are very frequent in the Close Reading paper (and in the Textual Analysis assessment), and, worryingly, they are often badly done, mainly because candidates do not know how to tackle them. A knowledge about grammar helps enormously because it gives you an analytical tool – a method by which you can tackle the sentence.

EXAM EXAMPLE 1

Let's take some examples, all from Close Reading past papers:

> *Yet Ireland has managed to attract its young entrepreneurs back to help drive a burgeoning economy. We must try to do likewise. We need immigrants. We cannot grow the necessary skills fast enough to fill the gap sites. We need people with energy and commitment and motivation, three characteristics commonly found among those whose circumstances prompt them to make huge sacrifices to find a new life.*

7 Further Features of Sentence Structure

The question was:

> **Show how the writer uses sentence structure to demonstrate her strength of feeling in the above paragraph.** [2 marks]

Note that the question is worth two marks, which means that we should make two points: first, we analyse the structure; then, secondly, go on to say how that structure demonstrates the strength of feeling. Let's list the devices along with an appropriate comment:

- Look again at the final three sentences of the extract: they increase in length, climaxing in the long final sentence, thus creating drama and emotion.
- Note the repetition of the *We + (verb)* at the beginning of each of these sentences – **parallel structure**, which in this case is a **rhetorical device**, the effect of which is to make the reader feel uplifted and involved in the writer's argument.
- The **parallel structure** of *We must.../We need.../We cannot...* is also, in this case, the language of passionate persuasion.
- The use of the short sentences in contrast with the long one creates impact and draws attention to the dramatic tone of the shorter ones.
- The final sentence is structured as a list and the repetition of the *and* means that it is an **asyndetic list**, creating a relentless build up or **climax** of enthusiasm while drawing attention to and emphasising the significance of each of the items in the list.

We have identified, then, five language devices in the two sentences of the extract and we have made comments on the effect of each – we have done much more than is required for two marks!

Let's have a closer look at the devices we identified. We shall start with the lists since you already know something about the use of lists.

Polysyndetic and asyndetic lists

A normal list inserts an *and* between the penultimate (second last) item and the last. Indeed, it is the use of the word *and* that draws the reader's or the listener's attention to the fact that the list is ending. But there are two other kinds of list which writers use: **polysyndetic lists**, which use many conjunctions and tend to have the effect of stressing each item, usually (as in the case above) as the list builds up to a climax. But the other kind of list is an **asyndetic list**,

44 *Higher English* Grade Booster

where there are no conjunctions, creating a much more haphazard, random effect. In Philip Larkin's poem *Mr Bleaney*, there is a list of objects in Mr Bleaney's room:

> *Bed, upright chair, sixty-watt bulb, no hook*
> *Behind the door, no room for books or bags*

Instantly, you see that it is an asyndetic list, which effectively creates a quick, random notion of the barrenness of the room, its lack of comfort, as well as the impression that it is devoid of any personality, like its previous tenant.

Increasing sentence length

We have already noted the final three sentences of the extract above:

> *We need immigrants. We cannot grow the necessary skills fast enough to fill the gap sites. We need people with energy and commitment and motivation, three characteristics commonly found among those whose circumstances prompt them to make huge sacrifices to find a new life*

They increase in length and that structure invariably creates the effect of build-up or **climax**.

Short and long sentences

Sometimes the structure of the sentence does not involve lists. Rather it is the use of a short sentence which makes a dramatic contrast to a longer sentence, thereby drawing attention to the meaning and dramatic impact of the shorter sentence.

Again, you should be aware in your own writing of the effect of varying sentence length: short sentences can be highly dramatic and can therefore reinforce meaning.

Link sentences

An important aspect of structure is the linking function a sentence – or a paragraph – can play. Paragraphs really ought to be linked: one paragraph of a piece of writing should follow on from the previous one, and often that link is by means of the structure of the first sentence of the following paragraph.

In the Close Reading paper there are frequently questions asked about the linking function of such a sentence. When you are asked to show how a sentence at the beginning of a paragraph acts as a link sentence between the paragraphs, then follow this procedure:

7 Further Features of Sentence Structure

- quote the word or words that link back – look for words such as 'these', 'all this', 'therein', 'therefore', etc;
- demonstrate the link back to the idea of the previous paragraph;
- quote the word or words that link forward to the idea of the new paragraph;
- demonstrate the link forward to that idea.

EXAM EXAMPLE 2

Again the following extract is taken from a Close Reading passage used in an actual SQA examination:

> Most of all the stuff earmarked for Waste Isolation Pilot Plant (WIPP) in the New Mexico desert is plutonium-contaminated detritus which emits relatively low quantities of radio activity – gloves, bits of drill, flasks, valves, rags, test-tubes, pipes, sludge, shoes, lab coats, and so on. But some of it is the most threatening material on earth. For this network of tunnelled-out salt corridors, 26 miles east of Carlsbad, is to become, if the US government has its way, home for all the radioactive garbage created by US weapons plants during the Cold War. This includes 24,000 soft steel 55-gallon caskets containing waste that can kill someone within half an hour of exposure. The material will be radioactive for at least 10,000 years and, in some cases, far longer.
>
> And therein lies the rub. Once the WIPP complex is filled, sometime in the next 50 years, the plant above ground will be vacated and returned to the desert. Its small clump of sand-coloured administration buildings, surrounded by barbed wire, and spotlights, will be removed.
>
> How, then, should the rulers of today warn future generations of the filthy brew that they have buried beneath their feet? How will they stop them digging into it?

The question that year was:

> **'And therein lies the rub.'** Explain how this sentence acts a link between the first paragraph and the two following paragraphs.
>
> [2 marks]

46 *Higher English* **Grade Booster**

Further Features of Sentence Structure

Simply follow the procedure outlined above (each point is worth a ½ mark):

- Quote the words that link back – in this case *And therein* because *And* is a linking word and *therein* refers to the idea that has gone before it. (To be very technical, words such as *this, that, these, those, therein* take **antecedents** – in other words they have to refer to something that has gone before.)
- Demonstrate the idea that the words link back to – in this case the words *And therein* link back to the idea in the previous paragraph that the material will be radioactive for at least 10 000 years.
- Quote the words that link forward – in this case *lies the rub* (which means that is where the problem lies – the phrase comes from *Hamlet* by Shakespeare).
- Demonstrate the idea(s) to which these words refer – in this case the idea that given that the contaminated waste is to be buried how will today's rulers warn future generations of its existence without arousing curiosity?

A good answer, then, might be:

> The word 'therein' (½ mark)
> refers to the idea at the end of the previous paragraph where the author has referred to the length of time that the material will remain radioactive (½ mark),
> while the phrase 'lies the rub' (½ mark)
> refers to the problems involved in warning future generations of its existence without arousing curiosity. (½ mark)

RHETORIC

Earlier in the chapter we saw an example of a **rhetorical device** (page 44). Rhetoric is a feature that we usually associate with speeches, where the speaker (or orator) uses language effectively to persuade or influence. Here are some features of rhetoric:

- **Repetition** – where, as in the case above, the beginnings of sentences are repeated to create a cumulative, dramatic – even passionate – effect;

Higher English Grade Booster 47

Further Features of Sentence Structure

- **Rhetorical question** – a question to which no answer is required or in which the answer is implied (e.g. *Who knows?* – the implication being *Nobody*); and
- **Prolepsis** – a device which anticipates an objection before it is made (e.g. *And before you say that…*).

In this, the 21st century, our contribution to the range of rhetorical devices is the **soundbite**, a short, snappy, quotable expression, much favoured by politicians. The idea is that their statement will appear in the following day's press. For example, Tony Blair's

> *We will fight crime and the causes of crime.*

Sometimes, however, we get the impression that these expressions are more style than substance: some soundbites sound significant but are, in fact, without much meaning.

> When you are asked to comment on sentence structure, remember the above examples. But if you have forgotten, say, the **asyndetic list**, just use your common sense: any linguistic device must support meaning, therefore clarify for yourself the meaning of the sentence and then examine how – in what way – the structure is supporting that meaning.

But you also must always remember that reading and writing are two sides of the same coin. The more you acquire knowledge and skills about writing techniques – such as, in this case, the skills involved in sentence structure – the more you must start to adopt them in your own writing. Writing skills have to be practised, and the more you practise using lists in your own writing, the more you will recognise and understand their effect in other people's writing. In a sense, all these devices contribute to a **rhythm** – and it is the rhythm that creates the dramatic, memorable effect. Therefore you should consider the opening sentence and the closing sentence of your own writing to see if you can improve the rhythm!

SOMETHING FOR YOU TO TRY

Try writing a paragraph, on any subject of your choice, where you employ a list – preferably a **polysyndetic list** – for dramatic effect.

EXAM EXAMPLE 3

The next example is from an SQA Textual Analysis assessment:

> Ahead of us, up some steps, around corners unseen, the Jaguar Throne crouches in a square cubicle, its ruby eyes glowing, its teeth vivid, its meaning lost. Who used it last, what was it for, why was it kept here, out of sight in the darkness?

The question was:

> **In what ways does sentence structure in the above paragraph contribute to the mysterious nature of the Jaguar Throne?**
> [4 marks]

Once again, the first step is to analyse the sentence structure (2 points = 2 marks) then go on to comment on how it contributes to the mysterious nature (2 points = 2 marks). Sometimes the comment is implied in or part of the analysis, and that is perfectly acceptable.

Answer:

> There are three **prepositional phrases** [see the table on page 32 and explanation on page 35] at the beginning of the first sentence – 'Ahead of us', 'up some steps', 'around corners unseen' and these in the form of a list have the effect of delaying the main verb expressing the idea of the Jaguar Throne crouching, thus creating climax and heightening the mystery (easily worth 4 marks: 2 for structure, 2 for effect). After the verb, there is another asyndetic list in parallel structure, each item of which builds up to the dramatic and mysterious 'its meaning lost'. The final sentence is a listing of questions – and the use of questions in itself contributes to and intensifies the idea of mystery – but here the list is also a dramatic build-up to the final 'in the darkness' (again, easily worth 4 marks).

When you are asked about sentence structure, your knowledge gained from chapters 3 and 4 will help you enormously. You know about **prepositional phrases**, **pre-modification** and **post-modification**, and about the various other features of sentence structure.

7 Further Features of Sentence Structure

EXAM EXAMPLE 4

Look at this next example, adapted from a previous SQA Close Reading paper:

> I remember as a boy being alone in the living-room of our council-house in Kilmarnock. I would be maybe 11 years old. I was lying in front of the coal-fire with my head resting on an armchair. It was, I think, late on a winter afternoon. The window had gone black and I hadn't put the light on, enjoying the small cave of brightness and heat the fire had hewn from the dark. Perhaps I was a far traveller resting by his camp-fire. Perhaps I was a knight keeping vigil for the dawn when wondrous deeds would be done. For I could be many people at that time as I still can.
>
> I don't know. I am simply aware of being there. The moment sits separate and vivid in my memory, without explanation, like a rootless flower. Whoever I was being, traveller or knight, I must have been tired. For I fell asleep.

Question:

> **By reference to sentence structure, show how in the second paragraph the writer reinforces the significance of the moment described in the previous paragraph.** [2 marks]

This time we are not really presented with lists, but we do notice that the sentences in the second paragraph are short and that is part of the answer.

Answer:

> The use of short sentences at the beginning of the second paragraph creates a dramatic effect and that in turn reinforces the moment as opposed to the speculation in the previous paragraph. The short sentences create a dramatic contrast with the longer ones and thereby draw attention to their significance (**easily worth 2 marks**). Moreover, the final short sentence creates an anti-climax and thereby draws attention to his falling asleep, thereby isolating the moment itself (**worth 2 marks**). Finally, the use of the series of short prepositional phrases in the third sentence – 'in my memory, without explanation, like a rootless flower' – reinforces the isolation and therefore the significance of the moment (**worth 2 marks**).

50 *Higher English* **Grade Booster**

Further Features of Sentence Structure

But you should also notice the switch in tense: the first paragraph is in the past tense, but the second paragraph is in the present tense – *I don't know* and *I am simply aware*. This switch to the present creates an impact reinforcing the significance of the moment – it is still with him.

> Always pay attention to any switch in tense.

> Once you know what to do, it is relatively easy to score the marks!

EXAMPLES FOR YOU TO TRY

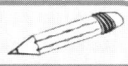

Comment fully on the effectiveness of the sentence structure of the following sentences. (You should try to make as many points as you can – identify structural points and comment on their effectiveness.)

1. On June 16, in a move calculated to humiliate and frighten the Mexican people, Cortez set fire to the aviaries.

2. I let go of the dog, and it galloped immediately to the back of the gallows; but when it got there it stopped short, barked, and then retreated into a corner of the yard, where it stood among the weeds, looking timorously out at us.

3. In one, sailors were singing at their work; in another, there were men aloft, high over my head, hanging to threads that seemed no thicker than a spider's.

4. I saw the most wonderful figure-heads, that had all been far over the ocean. I saw, besides, many old sailors, with rings in their ears, and whiskers curled in ringlets, and tarry pigtails, and their swaggering, clumsy sea-walk; and if I had seen as many kings or arch-bishops I could not have been more delighted.

5. To strive, to seek, to find, and not to yield.

7 Further Features of Sentence Structure

ANOTHER EXAMPLE FOR YOU TO TRY

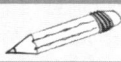

Read carefully the following two paragraphs:

Nor is it easy to see how you ensure that any sizeable monument, however forbidding, will not fill gold-diggers or future archaeologists with such curiosity that they start digging underneath it. Over the ages, few historic sites have been spared intrusion from bounty-hunters, vandals or prying scholars. Worse, the dump lies in an area of south-eastern New Mexico which is dotted with oil and hydrogen wells, and basalt mines. A prospector could happen upon its contents while boring for minerals.

To tackle these issues, the Sandia National Laboratory in Albuquerque, the nuclear weapons development and research agency, convened a panel of 13 experts. They included anthropologists, materials scientists, astronomers, a psychologist, an architect and a linguist. Their deliberations were closely followed by nuclear regulatory agencies worldwide, including Britain's. It was the first time anyone, anywhere, had explored the issue in detail.

Explain how the first sentence of the second paragraph acts as a link between the two paragraphs.

8 Punctuation

The apostrophe
The plural in English
Examples for you to try
The comma splice
Punctuation marks
Exam examples 1–2
An example for you to try
Spelling

Many people claim that there are 'rules' concerning punctuation, that a comma is there to allow a pause or to enable the reader to take a breath. Nonsense. There are no 'rules' as such, only conventions, which ebb and flow on the tide of linguistic fashion. Today, for example, Lewis Grassic Gibbon would be chastised for his overuse of the **comma splice** (see pages 56–57) and Jane Austen's overlong sentences would be regarded as entirely unfashionable.

> There is only one thing you need to know about punctuation: its sole purpose is to clarify meaning.

THE APOSTROPHE

A writer's lack of punctuation or misuse of punctuation can cause ambiguity at best and confusion at worst. For example, the sign designers at the new parliament building at Holyrood decided, in their wisdom, to abolish the apostrophe because, they apparently claimed, it causes confusion, especially among the partially sighted. Maybe they felt that it is terribly 21st century to do away with it. Fair enough: we can all understand 'Gents Toilets' and even 'Ladies Restrooms'. But what about 'Members Lounge' – is that for one member or all members? The sign doesn't tell you. We are so familiar with 'Gents Toilets' that we know the abbreviation stands for 'Gentlemen's' – the plural of the noun. The spelling of 'Ladies' informs us that the restrooms are for more than one lady. But 'Members Lounge': how many dare enter? Were it signed using the apostrophe – 'Members' Lounge' – the position of the apostrophe signals that the word is plural and that therefore the lounge is for all members of the Scottish Parliament.

> Lesson Number 1, then, about the apostrophe is that it is *extremely useful*.

> Lesson Number 2 is that *you shouldn't be afraid of the apostrophe!*

The apostrophe is used:

- when a word is contracted (shortened) – the apostrophe indicates that a letter is missing (e.g. *isn't* for *is not*, *it's* for *it is*, *mustn't* for *must not*); and
- when the writer wants to indicate possession (e.g. *the boy's book* for *the book belonging to the boy* and *the girl's CD* for *the CD belonging to the girl*).

> When it comes to possession, the rule could not be simpler: the apostrophe always goes before the *–s* except in the plural when the plural is formed by adding an *–s*, in which case the apostrophe comes after the *–s*.

THE PLURAL IN ENGLISH

In English, we can form the plural in several ways:

- by adding *–s* to the singular as in dog/dogs;
- by adding *–es* to the singular as in church/churches or box/boxes;

Punctuation

- by changing –*f* to –*ves* as in loaf/loaves or thief/thieves or hoof/hooves, though *chief, roof* and *reef* form the plural by adding only –*s*. Where the vowel is short (that is, pronounced *eh* and not *ee*) the plural is formed by adding an –*s* as in chef/chefs;
- by changing the last letter *y* of a word and adding –*ies* – as in lady/ladies or army/armies;
- by changing the vowel – as in man/men or mouse/mice;
- by adding an *n* or an *en* – as in ox/oxen or child/children;
- by altering nothing – as in sheep/sheep or deer/deer.

> Remember: the apostrophe always comes before the –*s* unless the plural is formed by adding an –*s* in which case it comes after the –*s*. With words such as **sheep** and **deer** (the plural of which is the same – **sheep, deer**) we would probably avoid the apostrophe altogether (e.g. **a deer forest** or **a field for sheep**).

Let's (short for *Let us*) set that out as a table:

SINGULAR – always the same way of forming the possessive		PLURAL – where the plural is formed by adding an *s*	
fox	fox's	bottles	bottles'
dog	dog's	dogs	dogs'
lady	lady's	ladies	ladies'
cat	cat's	cats	cats'
SINGULAR – always the same way of forming the possessive		**PLURAL – where the plural is formed by changing the vowel**	
man	man's	men	men's
woman	woman's	women	women's
SINGULAR – always the same way of forming the possessive		**PLURAL – where the plural is formed by adding an *n***	
child	child's	children	children's
ox	ox's	oxen	oxen's

Punctuation

> A simple way of remembering how to use the apostrophe where it indicates possession: insert the apostrophe followed by an *s* except when the plural already ends in an *s*, in which case simply add the apostrophe.

EXAMPLES FOR YOU TO TRY

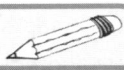

the coat belonging to the boy

the scarf belonging to the girl

the pullover belonging to the man

the cars belonging to the men

the dresses belonging to the ladies

the ploughs belonging to the oxen

the shoes belonging to the aliens

the tickets belonging to the senior citizens

the candy floss belonging to the children

the money belonging to the bank manager

the ship belonging to the captain

the computer belonging to the mother

the newspapers belonging to the men

> Watch the word *it*: the possessive is *its* - the word *its* is already possessive. *It's* stands for *it is*.

THE COMMA SPLICE

Apart from the mistakes with the apostrophe, the other most common mistake is what has come to be called the **comma splice**. The comma cannot be used to join clearly related units of sense in one sentence.

For example, many people are tempted to write:

I have a dog, its name is Mandy.

Although *I have a dog* and *its name is Mandy* are two clearly related units of sense, nevertheless they cannot be joined together (or spliced) by a comma. Obviously, to leave these units of sense as two separated sentences would create a style that is almost childish:

I have a dog. Its name is Mandy.

There are, however, other ways in which these two units of sense can be joined:

- use a **conjunction** (see table on page 32) – *I have a dog and its name is Mandy*;
- use a **relative pronoun** (see table on page 30) – *I have a dog **whose** name is Mandy.*

But by far the most stylish method of joining these two units of sense is to use the **semi-colon**:

- use a **semi-colon** (see table below) – *I have a dog; its name is Mandy.*

> The semi-colon is a much neglected, underused, and yet most sophisticated of punctuation marks – its use will give your writing maturity and style.

It is also a punctuation mark the use of which is frequently the subject of a question in Close Reading.

PUNCTUATION MARKS

Now let us look at all the punctuation marks that you need to know.

> Try to remember that punctuation is always used to clarify meaning for or to signal meaning to the reader.

Higher English **Grade Booster** 57

Punctuation

Punctuation mark	Example	Explanation of usage
Comma ,	This number is being played live, in response to many requests, by Robbie Williams.	*Used to clarify the text and avoid ambiguity (without the second comma it could mean that Robbie Williams made the request)*
	Hello, George, how are you?	*Used (as a pair of commas) when addressing someone (sometimes known as the **vocative of address**)*
	I went to the shop, the one on the corner, to get coffee.	*Used (as a pair of commas) round **parenthesis***
	Brad Pitt, world famous movie star, has just arrived in Britain.	*Used (as a pair of commas) round **apposition** (see page 34)*
	Bed, upright chair, sixty-watt bulb, no hook / Behind the door, no room for books or bags.	*Used to separate items in a list*
	In the morning, I shall go to university.	*To separate a prepositional phrase when it is out of normal sequence*
Colon :	See following example. *The alternatives included:* and the list follows…	*To introduce a list*
	The isle is the most desolate place I have ever seen: its docks deserted, windows smashed, walls spray-gunned.	*To signal an explanation following a statement*
	To err is human: to forgive divine.	*To contribute to the balance of a sentence which contains contrasting ideas (rare)*

58 *Higher English* **Grade Booster**

Punctuation

Punctuation mark	Example	Explanation of usage
Semi-colon (;)	I have a dog; her name is Mandy	*To indicate an interconnection between items which in themselves could stand as grammatically independent sentences*
	'The alternatives included: a "Landscape of Thorns" – a square mile of randomly-spaced 80 ft spikes; "Menacing Earthworks" – giant mounds surrounding a 2,000 ft map of the world displaying all of the planet's nuclear waste dumps; a "Black Hole" – a huge slab of black concrete that absorbs so much solar heat theat it is impossible to approach	*To separate items in a complex list where commas are already used within items*
Single dash (—)	My brother went to work today – or was it yesterday?	*To indicate an afterthought*
	'Landscape of Thorns' – a square mile of randomly-spaced 80 ft spikes	*More recently, to replace the colon after a statement and before the explanation.*
	'Menacing Earthworks' – giant mounds surrounding a 2,000 ft map of the world displaying all the planet's nuclear waste dumps	
	'Black Hole' – a huge slab of black concrete that absorbs so much solar heat that it is impossible to approach	

Higher English **Grade Booster** 59

Punctuation

Punctuation mark	Example	Explanation of usage
Paired dash and Paired brackets Paired comma (Parenthesis)	I often go to the disco – the one off Union Street – on Friday evenings. Or I met Kevin at the disco last night (he often goes there on Fridays) and he told me about the strangest happening.	*To isolate information which is additional to the sentence but grammatically separate from it*
Inverted commas ' ' or " "	'Hello, Martha,' said Julian, 'how are you today?' 'To be or not to be'. 'Macbeth' It was hardly the 'experiment' he had hoped for.	*To indicate the words actually used by a speaker in direct speech* *To indicate the words of a quotation* *To indicate the titles of books, plays, films, etc.* *To indicate a word used in an unusual way or slightly out of context*
Apostrophe '	don't can't John's book	*To denote the contraction of a word by the omission of a letter or letters* *To indicate possession*
Aposiopesis ...	The three dots at the end of a sentence…	*A device to indicate the sudden breaking off of speech or line of thought; or indicating a trailing off, the line of thought implied rather than expressed; or a change in subject; or an unwillingness to continue*

60 *Higher English* **Grade Booster**

Punctuation

Punctuation mark	Example	Explanation of usage
Ellipsis ...	The three dots in the middle of a sentence 'To be, or not to be, that is the question / Whether 'tis nobler in the mind…end them.'	A device to indicate that some words have been missed out
Question mark ?	'Is this a dagger I see before me?' Who do you think you are?	Indicates the interrogative or question. Can create a questioning tone or doubt Can indicate a rhetorical question – one the answer to which is understood or implied
Exclamation mark !	Hello! Watch out! Careful! Take care! Stop! Slow down! Hurry up! Danger!	Indicates surprise or a command or warning – used in road signs to indicate danger
Full stop .	It marks the end of a sentence.	Not to be confused with the comma
Capital letters	Mark the beginning of a sentence and are used to indicate a proper noun, even when abbreviated to its initial letters	The dog crossed the road. Kevin. Australia. Scotland. Edinburgh. Macbeth. British Broadcasting Corporation (BBC)

The table above is intended as a guideline: always remember that there are no hard and fast rules regarding punctuation. Use your common sense to work out in what way(s) a given punctuation mark is clarifying or signalling meaning.

Higher English **Grade Booster**

8 Punctuation

EXAM EXAMPLE 1

Read carefully the following extract – taken from a past SQA paper:

> *The scientists say that even if the world's governments and industries meet international goals on reducing greenhouse gasses – which they probably will not – it still won't be enough to prevent severe changes to the world's weather. Their advice to governments, business and private citizens about this is grim: get used to it.*

The question that year was straightforward enough:

> **Show how the writer helps to clarify his meaning by using:**
> **(i) dashes; and (ii) a colon.**

Remember to examine *how* the punctuation is working.

(i) Look at the dashes: *even if the world's governments and industries meet international goals on reducing greenhouse gasses – which they probably will not – it still won't be enough to prevent severe changes to the world's weather.* You are right to spot the parenthesis: the clause *which they probably will not* is additional information which is not grammatically part of the sentence but is an aside, presenting or drawing attention to what the author sees as the reality of the situation or what is most likely to be the outcome of the situation.

(ii) Now look at the use of the colon – *Their advice to governments, business and private citizens about this is grim: get used to it.* This isn't the traditional statement and explanation, though in a sense it is an explanation of the advice, while (more importantly) signalling the main message.

EXAM EXAMPLE 2

Read carefully the following extract from a passage used in the Higher. It has been adapted from the introduction to *I'm a Little Special – A Muhammed Ali Reader*. Gerald Early considers his reactions to Ali's conviction for dodging the draft for the Vietnam War:

> *I drifted away from baseball by steps and bounds. The next summer, 1967, Ali was convicted of draft dodging. Martin Luther King came out against the Vietnam War. Baseball did not seem very important. Something else was. For you see, I could never be sure, before that spring when Ali first refused to be*

drafted, if in the end he really would refuse an unjust fight. So when he did finally refuse, I felt something greater than pride: I felt as though my honour as a black boy had been defended, my honour as a human being. He was the grand knight, after all, the dragon slayer. And I felt myself, little inner-city boy that I was, his apprentice to the grand imagination, the grand daring. The day that Ali refused the draft, I cried in my room. I cried for him and for myself, for my future and his, for all our black possibilities. If only I could sacrifice like that, I thought. If only I could sacrifice my life like Muhammed Ali...

The question that year was:

> **Show how the writer's language in the final paragraph** (all of the above) **conveys the passion he felt about Ali's decision not to fight in the Vietnam War. In your answer you should refer to more that one of the following: imagery, sentence structure, punctuation, word choice.** (4 marks)

Now we will look at imagery and word choice later in this book, but at the moment you can answer the question by referring solely to sentence structure and punctuation.

Let's begin with sentence structure (any one of the explanations below is worth two marks):

- First, there is the use of the list – *The next summer, 1967, Ali was convicted of draft dodging. Martin Luther King came out against the Vietnam War. Baseball did not seem very important. Something else was.* The list delivers a climax, culminating in the fact that baseball was no longer important to the author.

- Secondly, there is the dramatic impact of the short sentence – *Something else was.* And this leads significantly to the next point the author is about to make.

- Thirdly, in the sentence – *And I felt myself, little inner-city boy that I was, his apprentice to the grand imagination, the grand daring* – there is the use of the And at the beginning of the sentence creating a dramatic link building to the climax at the end of the sentence – *the grand daring* – a climax made all the more dramatic by the delay created by the parenthesis *little inner-city boy that I was*.

- Fourthly, there is the repetition of *I cried* – *I cried in my room. I cried for him and for...* and the repetition of *If only I could sacrifice* in the last two sentences. Both these repetitions (a kind of parallel structure) create a rhetorical device building up a feeling of passion in the writing.

Punctuation

Now let us examine the punctuation – again any of the points below is worth two marks:

- First, there is the classic use of the **colon** – *I felt something greater than pride: I felt as though my honour as a black boy had been defended, my honour as a human being* – which is used to indicate the explanation after a statement. The explanation is dramatic and forceful, contributing to the strength of feeling in the writing.
- Secondly, there is the **aposiopesis** (the three dots) at the very end, suggesting a trailing off, the continuing line of thought implied but not expressed, thus, in a sense, heightening the feeling.

AN EXAMPLE FOR YOU TO TRY

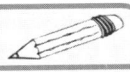

Read carefully the following passage, again from an actual SQA paper:

When we are old there is more time for gossiping (men talk and discuss: women gossip, don't they?). I see old women together arm in arm negotiating a slippery pavement or rough steps. I see them with their trolleys gossiping together in the supermarket and I rejoice that we have each other, that the older we grow the more women of our own age there are around us. We are not going to be identified as a 'growing social problem', as the social commentators would have us labelled, but as a thriving, gossiping and defiant sisterhood.

The question that year was:

> **How does the writer use sentence structure and punctuation in the above paragraph to make clear her point of view?**
>
> [4 marks]

One example of sentence structure and one of punctuation plus appropriate comment would be enough to score the four marks, but you should try to identify two examples of sentence structure and two of punctuation with appropriate comment!

SPELLING

You need to be able to spell accurately the following words (you may also need to consult a dictionary for the meaning of some!):

necessary	unnecessary	embarrass	loneliness	safely
business	benefited	dramatic	tragedy	livelihood
commit	committed	commitment	accommodation	skilful
beautiful	spoonful	opposite	century	narrative
occasion	occasionally	referring	profession	impenetrable
sarcasm	dining room	emphasis	literature	criticism
character	scene	explanation	panicked	beginning
occurred	omission	omit	argument	extremely
rhythm	rhyme	soliloquy	participle	principal
definite	definitely	indefinitely	subtly	subtle
immorality	develop	development	interest	refer
reference	relevant	irrelevant	immediate	immediately
controversy	medicine	disapproval	conjures	in fact
all right	circumstances	comment	there (place)	their (possession)
privilege	guarantee	responsibility	recently	hurriedly
intimidating	supposedly	until	forget	across
completely	vigorously	humorously		
pierce	tendency	tendentious		
sentence	sententious	pretentious		
graffiti	occurring	discreet (meaning unobtrusive)		
discreetly	discrete (meaning separate)	discretely		
epitome				

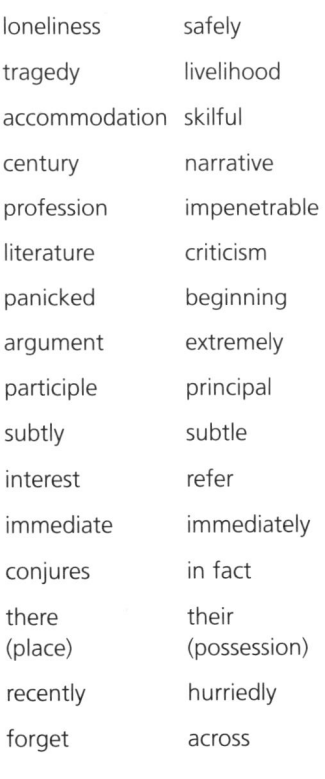

8 Punctuation

The following are some guidelines to help you spell more accurately:

(1) With words which have **prefixes** and/or **suffixes**, add the prefix and/or suffix to the stock word – and this will help your spelling. Thus:

Dis	+	appear	=	disappear
Dis	+	solve	=	dissolve
Im	+	mediate	=	immediate
Im	+	moral	=	immoral
Im	+	proper	=	improper

(2) There are, as you know, five vowel sounds in English – *a, e, i, o* and *u*. We can pronounce those vowels as in *hate, feed, pine, slope* and *cute*. The sounds produced in pronouncing the vowels in this way are known as *long vowel sounds*. We can, however, also pronounce these same vowels with a *short vowel sound* as in *hat, fed, pin, slop* and *cut*. Now, in words ending in – ing, where the vowel before the –ing is short, the consonant is doubled. The rule isn't 100% foolproof, but it is a good guide. Thus:

dine (drop the e)	+			ing	=	dining room
begin	+	n	+	ing	=	beginning
spin	+	n	+	ing	=	spinning
refer	+	r	+	ing	=	referring
twin	+	n	+	ing	=	twinning
pine (drop the e)	+			ing	=	pining
line (drop the e)	+			ing	=	lining
sneak	+			ing	=	sneaking

(3) In a two syllable word, where the second syllable is weak (i.e. not stressed when you pronounce the word), do not double the consonant before adding *–ing*. For example:

In the word *snigger*, the *–er* is weak, the stress comes on the first syllable, therefore keep the *r* single.
In the word *benefit*, the *–fit* is weak, therefore the *t* remains single.
Similarly, in the word *target* the *–et* is weak, therefore the *t* remains single.
But in *omit*, the *–it* is stressed therefore you have to double the consonant – i.e. *omitting*.

(4) Remember the old rule: *i* before *e* except after *c*, with certain exceptions such as *seize, weigh, beige, caffeine, eight, Neil, Sheila…*

9 Imagery, Word Choice, Tone and Conclusions

Connotation and denotation

Exam examples 1–3

Questions about tone

Exam example 4

Conclusions

Exam example 5

The other kinds of questions that can be asked in Close Reading and in Textual Analysis are questions about imagery and word choice.

CONNOTATION AND DENOTATION

Let's begin with the word *connotation*. Words in English have two levels of meaning – *denotation* and *connotation*. The **denotation** of a word is the object in the universe to which the word refers – i.e. pen, laptop, orange, Mars, Venus – when the writer or speaker is referring to an actual pen, laptop, or orange. The **connotation** of a word is the associations we have for a word – all the things that the word suggests to us, its appeal to our imagination. For example, the word *apple* can suggest adjectives such as *crisp, juicy, red, luscious, sweet* or it can suggest ideas such as *worm* (apples do sometimes have worms in them!) or even can allude (**allusions** are references to other literary or biblical works) to the Adam and Eve story.

The word *bar* could suggest *chocolate, a prison, a piece of iron, a pub, an ingot of gold, a gymnasium* (wall bars). But the **context** of a sentence in which the word appears will apply a constraint on its connotation (sometimes referred to as the *connotative area* of a word). For example, take the sentence:

> *I went into the bar and bought a drink.*

9 Imagery, Word Choice, Tone and Conclusions

Here the word *bar* cannot suggest chocolate, but will suggest a pub: the word group *bought* a *drink* restricts the connotation to a pub, just as the word *bar* suggests that the drink is in all probability an alcoholic one.

The kind of questions that you are likely to be asked in the Close Reading paper are:

> **By reference to word choice show how the writer expresses disapproval**

or

> **What mood or atmosphere has been created by the writer and show how this mood or atmosphere has been created – you should refer to word choice in your answer.**

There is a way of answering such questions. You first of all have to refer to the relevant words then, going by the connotations of these words within the context, show how the approval or tone has been created. Let's take an actual example:

EXAM EXAMPLE 1

Here once again is the Muhammed Ali passage which we looked at on page 62:

> *I drifted away from baseball by steps and bounds. The next summer, 1967, Ali was convicted of draft dodging. Martin Luther King came out against the Vietnam War. Baseball did not seem very important. Something else was. For you see, I could never be sure, before that spring when Ali first refused to be drafted, if in the end he really would refuse an unjust fight. So when he did finally refuse, I felt something greater than pride: I felt as though my honour as a black boy had been defended, my honour as a human being. He was the grand knight, after all, the dragon slayer. And I felt myself, little inner-city boy that I was, his apprentice to the grand imagination, the grand daring. The day that Ali refused the draft, I cried in my room. I cried for him and for myself, for my future and his, for all our black possibilities. If only I could sacrifice like that, I thought. If only I could sacrifice my life like Muhammed Ali…*

The question was:

Imagery, Word Choice, Tone and Conclusions

> **Show how the writer's language in the final paragraph** (all of the above) **conveys the passion he felt about Ali's decision not to fight in the Vietnam War. In your answer you should refer to more that one of the following: imagery, sentence structure, punctuation, word choice.** (4 marks)

We looked at sentence structure and punctuation on pages 63 and 64. Now is the time to look at imagery and word choice!

The task is to examine the word choice to show how the writer conveys the passion he felt about Ali's decision not to fight in the Vietnam War. We shall take it stage by stage:

- First, the word *drifted* suggests that baseball was no longer important to the writer – he simply lost interest in it because there were more important issues emerging for him.
- Secondly, the term *convicted of draft-dodging* has connotations of disobeying the law, of someone lacking in patriotism, of someone weak and cowardly; but the word group *came out against* in the next statement *Martin Luther King came out against the Vietnam War* suggests a moral stance, a declaration and support for Ali thus conveying the writer's strength of encouragement for Ali's position.
- Thirdly, the expression *unjust fight* makes clear the writer's point of view that the war was wrong and morally indefensible.
- Fourthly, *I felt something greater than pride* and *honour as a black boy* and *honour as a human being* are expressions which convey a sense of moral worth which is greater than mere strength of feeling. (Note that we are commenting on the connotations of words such as 'honour': any talk of the repetition of the word is a feature of sentence structure, not word choice!)
- Fifthly, expressions such as *the grand knight* and *the dragon-slayer* creates an image of medieval heroism, where the distinctions between right and wrong were never blurred. It also suggests something heroic about Ali – he is the force for good and moral uprightness who vanquishes evil.
- Sixthly, the word *apprentice* suggests that the writer was learning from the master – Ali.
- Finally, the word *sacrifice* has almost religious connotations, suggesting that there are higher ideals than mere existence.

See how easy it is! The problem is that candidates often perform badly in word choice/imagery questions simply because they are not sure what to do. Now any

9 Imagery, Word Choice, Tone and Conclusions

two of the above answers would earn all 4 marks – and you can now attempt word choice, sentence structure, and punctuation!

EXAM EXAMPLE 2

Remember the extract on page 46? Here it is again:

> Most of all the stuff earmarked for Waste Isolation Pilot Plant (WIPP) in the New Mexico desert is plutonium-contaminated detritus which emits relatively low quantities of radio activity – gloves, bits of drill, flasks, valves, rags, test-tubes, pipes, sludge, shoes, lab coats, and so on. But some of it is the most threatening material on earth. For this network of tunnelled-out salt corridors, 26 miles east of Carlsbad, is to become, if the US government has its way, home for all the radioactive garbage created by US weapons plants during the Cold War. This includes 24,000 soft steel 55-gallon caskets containing waste that can kill someone within half an hour of exposure. The material will be radioactive for at least 10,000 years and, in some cases, far longer.
>
> And therein lies the rub. Once the WIPP complex is filled, sometime in the next 50 years, the plant above ground will be vacated and returned to the desert. Its small clump of sand-coloured administration buildings, surrounded by barbed wire, and spotlights, will be removed
>
> How, then, should the rulers of today warn future generations of the filthy brew that they have buried beneath their feet? How will they stop them digging into it?

The question was:

> **How effective do you find the metaphor 'filthy brew'?**

'Metaphor?' I hear you ask. You may know the word but may not be entirely sure about metaphors. Well, the idea of metaphor is really very straightforward.

> A metaphor (and a simile) are devices of comparison.

You are invariably asked how effective you find a given metaphor. In which case there are a number of points to bear in mind and a system to work out effectiveness.

70 *Higher English* **Grade Booster**

Imagery, Word Choice, Tone and Conclusions

- To work out whether a metaphor is effective, work out whether it is appropriate. If it is appropriate, then it is effective.
- When working out if it is appropriate, follow the rules below:

Consider the metaphor: *Alistair was a lion in the fight*

1. Call the subject *Term A* and the thing to which the subject is being compared *Term B*.

2. Set out the sentence as follows – then work out the **connotations** of Term B. In this case, what comes into our minds when we think of lions? They are fierce, brave, ferocious, big, huge fangs, claws, strong, determined, courageous. Now ask yourself: which of these lion-like features would apply to someone who fought like a lion? If Alistair had great big fangs, that might apply, but claws?

   Now let's consider the features that are appropriate:

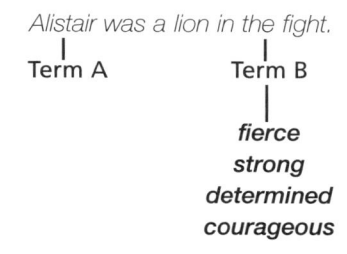

   Alistair was a lion in the fight.
   | |
   Term A   Term B
              |
              fierce
              strong
              determined
              courageous

   We know, then, that Alistair fought, *fiercely, strongly, determinedly, courageously.*

3. You can now say whether or not the metaphor is effective. If Alistair did not fight with ferocity, strength, determination, and courage, then the metaphor is *not* appropriate. If, however, that is how he fought, then the metaphor is appropriate, therefore it is effective.

4. Now let's try the one above from the Close Reading paper: *How effective do you find the metaphor 'filthy brew'?* Remember the sentence: *How, then, should the rulers of today warn future generations of the filthy brew that they have buried beneath their feet?*

   Which is Term A? The nuclear waste buried beneath the desert. Term B? The filthy brew. Let's analyse the metaphor:

9 Imagery, Word Choice, Tone and Conclusions

The nuclear waste is a filthy brew
  Term A   Term B

toxic
something mixed together
lethal
something fermenting
something poisonous produced by witches

In other words, we have examined the connotations of *filthy brew* and now we have to ask if those connotations are appropriate: do they apply to the nuclear waste buried underground? Of course they do. Therefore the metaphor is effective.

Your answer, then, might be:

> The metaphor 'filthy brew' is effective because it suggests a lethal concoction fermenting (underground), the kind of toxic mixture associated with witches, that will prove not only disgusting but utterly poisonous to mankind.

If you know what to do, as with everything in Close Reading and Textual Analysis, the question is easy to answer.

> When considering **Term B**, think of what the object looks like, smells like, tastes like, sounds like, feels like to the touch. Not all will be appropriate, but each is worth considering.

> Connotations (of word choice, metaphors, imagery in general) involve the five senses as well as the imagination.

But we need have a look at more examples of questions about word choice and imagery.

Imagery, Word Choice, Tone and Conclusions

EXAM EXAMPLE 3

Read the following, an extract from the passage of a very recent Close Reading past paper, in which the writer, Melanie Reid, expresses her concerns about the overprotection of children:

> I mourn also for the kids who will never know the delight of cycling with the wind in their hair, or climbing up trees, or exploring hidden places. Growing up devoid of freedom, decision-making, and the opportunity to learn from taking their own risks, our children are becoming trapped, neurotic, and as genetically weakened as battery hens.

The question was:

> **How effective do you find the image of 'battery hens' in conveying the writer's view of the way children are currently being brought up?**

Remember the system? Term A is the way in which children are being brought up and Term B is the image *battery hens*. So: what are the connotations of *battery hens*? The image suggests that hens are reared – as opposed to being 'brought up' – in a highly restricted and controlled environment, too close to each other to be healthy, in a way that most of us think is cruel. Are those features of battery-hen life appropriate, given the writer's argument that today's children are being denied the delights of freedom and risk-taking? Since the question is *How effective do you find...?* It is perfectly legitimate to say that you do not find the image effective, that you find it **clichéd**. But if you do that you have to show in what way it is clichéd. In this case it is easier to argue that it is entirely appropriate and therefore effective. Not only that, but the full image is *as genetically weakened* which suggests that there is less hope for future generations since this generation is being denied freedom to explore.

QUESTIONS ABOUT TONE

These are among the worst attempted questions in the whole of Higher English Close Reading and Textual Analysis. Yet they are really word choice questions in that tone is a product of the words used. If, as a writer, I want to create a dull,

9 Imagery, Word Choice, Tone and Conclusions

depressing tone, I am hardly going to open my short story on a beautiful, sunny paradise island! Rain can suggest a depressing sad tone, whereas sunshine can still create a happy tone, and snow a sparkly, tinsel tone.

That of course is a bit of an oversimplification. The following paragraph is from *Heart Songs*, a short story by E Annie Proulx:

> *The house was on a lake, and as he coasted down the drive, lined with its famous sixty-year-old blue Atlas cedars, he could see light from the living room window falling on the water like spilled oil. The car ticked hotly as he stood in the darkness. Under the slap of the waves against the dock he caught the monotonous pitch of mechanical television voices, and went inside.*

What is the tone of this paragraph? It sounds happy, calm, and optimistic with expressions such as *The house was on a lake, coasted down the drive, lined with its famous sixty-year-old blue Atlas cedars, light from the living room window,* and *slap of the waves* – all suggesting harmony and tranquillity, associated with the peace of a rural scene; but other expressions such as *falling on the water like spilled oil, The car ticked hotly, darkness, monotonous pitch,* and *mechanical television voices* suggest, on the contrary, the intrusion of an urban, technological disharmony and discord. The idyllic image of the lake (rural) is polluted by the spillage of oil (urban) and the pleasant sound of the waves is also spoiled by the harsh and boring sound of the voices from the television.

> Note that it is not enough merely to quote the appropriate words – you MUST comment on the way(s) in which the words suggest the tone. Thus *lake* suggests a peaceful rural setting whereas the expression *mechanical television voices* suggests something technical, intrusive, uncreative and boring.

Again, it is easier to explain more about tone using examples from the actual Higher.

EXAM EXAMPLE 4

The extract from the passage by Melanie Reid (page 73), continues:

> *I am fed up listening to scaremongers about the E-coli virus, telling me my child should never visit a farm or come into contact with animals. I am weary of organisations that are dedicated to promulgating the idea that threats and dangers to children lurk everywhere. I am sick of charities who on the one hand attack overprotective parents and at the same time say children should never be left unsupervised in public places.*

Imagery, Word Choice, Tone and Conclusions

Everywhere you turn there is an army of professionals – ably abetted by the media – hard at work encouraging parents to fear the worst. Don't let your children out in the sun – not unless they are wearing special UV-resistant T-shirts. Don't buy your child a Wendy house, they might crush their fingers on the hinges. Don't buy a baby walker, your toddlers might brain themselves. Don't buy plastic baby teethers, your baby might suck in harmful chemicals. Don't let them use mobile phones, they'll sizzle their brains. Don't buy a second-hand car seat, it will not protect them. And on and on it goes.

The candidates were told to read both paragraphs. The question then came in two parts:

> **(a) (i) Identify the tone of both paragraphs** [1 mark]
> **(ii) Explain how the tone is conveyed** [2 marks]
> **(b) How does the language of the second paragraph emphasise the writer's feelings about the 'army of professionals'?**
> **In your answer you should refer to at least two techniques such as sentence structure, tone, word choice.** [4 marks]

> You can see right away that this question is worth 7 marks or 14% of the available marks for the entire Close Reading – get the question right and that alone could make a difference to your final grade. That year the total marks for word choice, imagery, and tone questions amounted to 21 marks or 42% of the Close Reading paper!

How do we answer the question?

(a) (i) Tone. That is fairly easy: the tone is obviously one of anger, annoyance, frustration, contempt.

(ii) How is this tone conveyed? The answer lies in word choice: expressions such as *I am fed up listening to scaremongers, I am weary of organisations, I am sick of charities* all suggest, not weariness and boredom, but sheer frustration at these organisations giving her advice. These expressions convey exaggeration to emphasise the point.

Other examples of word choice are the expressions such as *scaremongers* which suggest people out to threaten and that angers her. Words such as *lurk* continue the idea of threat; *attack* and *army* suggest organised aggression; *abetted* suggests almost criminal conspiracy; *to fear the worst*

9 Imagery, Word Choice, Tone and Conclusions

suggests again the idea of overwhelming threat; *special UV-resistant T-shirts* suggests a sarcastic tone – and sarcasm is often related to annoyance or anger; *brain themselves, suck in harmful chemicals, sizzle their brains* all suggest the underlying violence of the threats. Other words, such as the repeated use of *never*, intensify the points that she is making and thus convey her anger. Even in the sentence – *I am sick of charities who on the one hand attack overprotective parents and at the same time say children should never be left unsupervised in public places* – the expression *on the one hand…at the same time* is an expression we normally use to achieve balance and here it draws attention to the contradictory, if not illogical, nature of the advice being offered.

Many, many points can be made from a huge selection of word choice, any one of which would earn full marks!

The repetition of the *I am fed up, I am weary*, and *I am sick of* is an entirely valid point about sentence structure and the comment would be about the way in which the repetition intensifies the tone considerably.

> **(b) how does the language of the second paragraph emphasise the writer's feelings about the 'army of professionals'.**

Because the question is about *language* and not specifically about word choice or imagery, then you can answer referring to punctuation and sentence structure as well as imagery and word choice. But we will begin with word choice.

Word choice: we have already used *army* and *abetted* but any reference can support more than one comment. This time the question is about how the language emphasises the writer's feelings about the army of professionals, therefore as long as your comments are directed to that you will be relevant. Let's try answering the question:

Word choice: The writer uses the word *army* with regard to *professionals* to suggest that their numbers are enormous, that they are highly trained and frightening. The word *abetted* used in relation to the media suggests that there is something conspiratorial and maybe even criminal about their activities.

Tone: the expression *ably abetted* is also sarcastic. She uses it to sneer at the *army of professionals*, while the expression *hard at work* is an example of **irony** in that she does not value their work in the slightest.

76 *Higher English* Grade Booster

Imagery, Word Choice, Tone and Conclusions

Expressions such as *brain themselves* and *sizzle their brains* are examples of highly **colloquial** language, used to convey a tone of sarcastic humour, poking fun at the *army of professionals*. The final short sentence *And on and on it goes* conveys a tone of mock weariness, a kind of frustration that has exhausted itself, at what she sees as the stupidity of the *army*.

Sentence structure: While we are at it we may as well look at how sentence structure emphasises the writer's feelings about the *army of professionals*. The parenthesis about the media – *ably abetted by the media* – draws attention to the sneering tone while the list of sentences in parallel structure, each beginning with *Don't*, each one an **imperative**, suggesting people don't do this, don't do that, draws attention to the authoritative, commanding attitude telling people what not to do. The very brevity of the final sentence *And on and on it goes*, along with the repetition of the *on and on*, creates a dismissive, curt attitude towards the *army of professionals*. It almost serves to trivialise what that army is all about.

> Remember: it is not enough to quote or make a reference: there are no marks available for references. You must make a comment. Sometimes your comments about sentence structure will overlap with tone – since sentence structure can contribute to tone – but that is acceptable.

CONCLUSIONS

There have been for years now questions about conclusions. The kind of question might be:

> **To what extent is the final paragraph an effective conclusion to the passage as a whole?**

> If the question is worded **To what extent**, you are free to argue that, in the above case, the final paragraph *is* or *is not* or *is only partially* an effective conclusion.

How do you answer such questions? First of all we need to know what makes an effective conclusion. There are four factors to consider:

Higher English Grade Booster

9   Imagery, Word Choice, Tone and Conclusions

- Look for words in the relevant paragraph (or sentence) which signal a conclusion or the idea of summing up. (Words such as *Thus...* or *Therefore it can be seen that...* or even *In conclusion...*)
- Look for sentence structure that creates climax – lists or delaying the main point to the very end or **alliteration** that creates a rhythm which suggests conclusion or climax.
- Look for a sentence or final sentences that are dramatic and memorable or humorous and memorable.
- Look for an **anecdote** or illustrative example which brings together the ideas that have been discussed in the passage.

EXAM EXAMPLE 5

Let's turn again to the passage about the Waste Isolation Pilot Plant (WIPP) on page 46. The passage is about the problem of alerting future generations over the next 10,000 years to the highly to nuclear waste buried under the desert in New Mexico. He makes the point in the passage that to communicate this a message over such a long period of time would be almost impossible. The passage ends:

> *The day after visiting WIPP, I flew back to Los Angeles. My taxi driver at the airport was from Lithuania, an erstwhile resident of the 'evil empire' that helped to generate the US nuclear weapons. I asked him to go to Encino, the neighbourhood where I live. 'Cinema?' he replied. I tried signs and gestures. Only after 15 minutes of garbled conversation did we straighten matters out. What chance would we have had, separated by 10,000 years?*

The question was:

> **By referring to the incident in the final paragraph, show how it is important in *two* ways to the passage as a whole.**

If you remember what we said about conclusions, this question becomes easy to answer. The paragraph illustrates the problem of communication – the misunderstanding/confusion of *cinema* with *Encino*. They sound the same, given that *Encino* is pronounced *Enseeno* and the Lithuanian taxi driver would have pronounced *cinema* as *seenema*. The dramatic yet humorous contrast of *15 minutes* and *10,000 years* further illustrates the impossibility of communication over a protracted period of time. The final dramatic sentence – *What chance would we have had, separated by 10,000 years?* – is made all the more

78 *Higher English* **Grade Booster**

Imagery, Word Choice, Tone and Conclusions

memorable by the fact that it is a **rhetorical question**.

By the very nature of this question, it is difficult to give worked examples. Clearly, to be able to evaluate the conclusion of a passage you would have to have read the entire passage, and space – or the lack of it – dictates the impossibility of reproducing such long texts. But remember the four points above – and that as well as word choice, tone, imagery, and anecdotes, you also should consider, if relevant, all that you know about sentence structure.

10 Literary Devices

Devices of comparison
Devices of representation
Devices of contrast
Devices of arrangement
Devices of sound
Other literary devices

There are many literary devices of which you should be aware. You need to know them, partly because you can be asked about some of them in Close Reading and Textual Analysis, but also because you should be able to refer to them in your Personal Study and Critical Essays.

We have already examined **metaphor** in detail – but there are many other devices – or figures of speech, as they used to be called. Here are the most important of them:

DEVICES OF COMPARISON

Metaphor – see pages 70–72

Personification – attributing human qualities and characteristics to inanimate objects. For example the bus, the destination board of which states: *I'm sorry, I'm not in service*. Clearly, buses are incapable of apology, but the personification is effective in that it is an attempt to give a bus a personality that is almost endearing when it is of no use to passengers.

Literary Devices

Simile – slightly weaker than metaphor in that Term A is not said to be Term B but is said to be *like* Term B. Similes use *like* or *as* to make the comparison. For example, *My love is like a red, red rose.* Like metaphor, a simile to be effective has to be appropriate.

Anthropomorphism – attributing human characteristics, feelings, attitudes, and qualities to animals. For example, *That sea-lion is clapping its hands!* Sea-lions don't have hands and they would not understand the concept of clapping, but the anthropomorphism makes the sea-lion out to be endearing and cute.

DEVICES OF REPRESENTATION

Metonymy – a much underrated literary device, the knowledge of which actually helps us analyse or **deconstruct** the ways in which some literature and films work. Metonymy is when we refer to some object or concept by something that can be seen to represent it. For example, in the law courts we refer to *The Crown versus Pat Bloggs*, where *The Crown* represents the state as embodied by Her Majesty – another metonymic symbol.

A perfect example of metonymy is the use of logos by companies and corporations. You all know what the British Petroleum logo is – BP in green and yellow. That logo – or metonymic image – represents all the values that British Petroleum claims it espouses. The image of a rose, for example, is not metaphoric – nothing is being compared – but a rose can represent love and lilies peace, just as red represents danger and green safety.

Metonymy is an important device used in films and television, where images tend to be representative rather than metaphoric. Some highly sophisticated television adverts exploit metonymic imagery, where a narrative can be used to represent the qualities of the brand being advertised – for example, recent Guinness and Stella Artois adverts which present stories almost unrelated to the products but which, nevertheless, represent aspects of them.

There is, however, another dimension to metonymy: many of you may well wear jeans or a T-shirt sporting a label you esteem – Nike, Adidas, Stone Island, Versace. Each of those companies will ensure that, displayed visibly on the garment, is the company's logo representing all that the company stands for – its values, its quality, its image. But by the same token, the fact that you are wearing it sends out a message representing you yourself – the image you want to portray to other people. Often we judge people in this shorthand way: the idea is not new since Shakespeare says in Hamlet that *apparel oft proclaims the man*. The clothes we wear often tell others something about ourselves.

We know that metonymy is important since companies and organisations spend millions of pounds in developing their logos!

Symbolism (symbols) – very similar to metonymy, but more specific. Flags are obvious examples of symbols since a flag symbolically represents a country and its values. Literature exploits symbolism, sometimes to **foreshadow** a story. Many novels, for example, begin with symbolic imagery, which, as we read on, can be seen to represent aspects of characterisation and/or **plot**. Sometimes symbols are used to create **mood** or **atmosphere** which, in itself, is in keeping with the story. Weather, for example, can be highly symbolic, with rain suggesting sadness.

Synecdoche – a type or subset of metonymy, where the part is used to represent the whole. For example, *A sail, a sail, I see a sail* where *sail* represents a ship. *They haven't even a roof over their heads* – where *roof* is used to represent shelter.

Transferred epithet – where we transfer an adjective which is usually associated with a human being to another object or idea. George Orwell talks about prisoners awaiting execution being in *condemned* cells, for example. It isn't the cell but the prisoner who is condemned. Wilfred Owen describes soldiers caught in a gas attack – *fitting the clumsy helmet just in time*. It's the men who are clumsy, not the helmet.

DEVICES OF CONTRAST

Oxymoron – the **juxtaposition** (the placing side by side) of opposites – often an adjective with a noun: for example, *bitter sweet, Parting is such sweet sorrow, idly busy*. What is effective about oxymoron is that both aspects are true: parting often is sorrowful but it is also sweet. One university currently advertises that its courses are *serious fun*.

Antithesis – a developed oxymoron, where the writer uses terms that are contrasted with each other. For example, *Better to reign in Hell than serve in Heaven* (John Milton) where not only Hell and Heaven are contrasted but also are *reign* and *serve*.

Epigram and paradox – an epigram is an apparent contradiction in language, which is effective because it is dramatic and therefore shocks the reader into attention. The contradiction, however, is not real. For example, *Great wits are sure to madness near allied* (John Dryden), *Brevity is the soul of wit* (Shakespeare). Paradox involves an actual contradiction, which nevertheless contains a grain of truth: *A favourite has no friend* (Thomas Gray), *He was conspicuous by his absence*.

Literary Devices

Paronomasia (pun) – where the writer uses the same word in different senses or when words have the same sound but different meanings: in the latter case *Portia* and *Porsche* sound the same but are totally different and in the former case, when Mercutio has been fatally wounded by Tybalt he says to Romeo, who has commented that the wound cannot be much, *Ask for me tomorrow, and you shall find me a grave man.* The effect is often to create a comic effect or **black humour**.

Zeugma (also known as syllepsis or condensed sentence) – where two words or ideas are linked together to create an anti-climactic or comic effect: *The last confetti and advice were thrown* (Philip Larkin), *She went home in a flood of tears and a taxi.*

DEVICES OF ARRANGEMENT

Climax – we have already examined climax as part of sentence structure – to have climax there has to be a list. But the point is also that in climax the list has to contain items in ascending order of importance such that the final item attracts most emphasis. Perhaps the most famous example of climax is from *Julius Caesar* by William Shakespeare, when Brutus, one of the (reluctant) conspirators who assassinated Caesar, says at his funeral: *As Caesar loved me, I weep for him; as he was fortunate, I rejoice at it; as he was valiant, I honour him; but as he was ambitious, I slew him.*

Anti-climax – anti-climax is not the reverse of climax – far from it. Anti-climax is where the least important idea comes at the end of the list. The most famous example of anti-climax is the lines by Alexander Pope from his *Rape of the Lock*:

> *Here thou, great Anna! Whom three realms obey,*
> *Dost sometimes counsel take – and sometimes tea.*

The effect is often humorous or intellectually appealing.

Bathos – accidental anti-climax, where the writer, invariably striving to be clever, unintentionally places the least important item last.

Inversion – an important poetic device linked to sentence structure. It is where the normal word order has been changed to create emphasis or formality. Look at these lines from *Church Going* by Philip Larkin. The persona (the person in the poem), an **agnostic**, has just visited an empty church, where he has related what he sees there in a light-hearted almost dismissive tone. The second verse ends:

> *Back at the door*
> *I sign the book, donate an Irish sixpence,*
> *Reflect the place was not worth stopping for.*

And the third verse begins

> *Yet stop I did: in fact, I often do*

Note the perfect use of inversion – the normal word order is *Yet I stopped*, but by inverting the word order, Larkin achieves a highly formal, poetic effect, contrasting strongly with the humorous, almost **colloquial** language of the previous verse. The reader then expects a change in **tone** to a more serious, reflective consideration of the subject.

Rhetorical question – again we examined rhetorical questions as part of sentence structure, but the important point to remember is that because the answer is obvious or implied, the device is used to draw the reader's attention to the point being made. A recent television advert used these lines by W.H. Davies:

> *What is this life, if full of care,*
> *We have no time to stand and stare?*

And Lady Macbeth's:

> *Yet who would have thought the old man to have had so much blood in him?*

DEVICES OF SOUND

Onomatopoeia – a device where the sound of word captures its sense. For example, *Crash! Boom!*

Alliteration – repetition of consonants to draw attention to meaning by the use of sound, to contribute to rhythm, to draw attention to the words themselves. For example, Wilfred Owen: *The rifles' rapid rattle* where the repetition of the *r* imitates the sound of rapid gun fire.

Assonance – the repetition of vowel sounds to draw attention to meaning by the use of sound, to contribute to rhythm, to draw attention to the words themselves – similar to alliteration! For example, Sylvia Plath at the beginning of *Daddy* writes:

You do not do, you do not do
Any more black shoe

The repetition of the *oo* sound captures a childish sound which supports the effect of the poem.

> A combination of certain repeated harsh vowel sounds with certain repeated ugly consonants can create extremely ugly sounds. It's no accident that our harshest swearing words use this combination of sounds!

OTHER LITERARY DEVICES

Irony – a device which is easier to recognise than define! It is where the writer draws attention to the meaning by apparently stating its opposite.

> Irony has to involve (a) a contrast in meaning, and (b) therefore an implied comment.

For example, in the Melanie Reid passage on page 75, she says:

Everywhere you turn there is an army of professionals – ably abetted by the media – hard at work encouraging parents to fear the worst.

We noted that the phrase – *hard at work* – is an example of irony because the implication is that she means the opposite – their work is not at all valued.

Sometimes irony simply involves the bringing together of two ideas or words or even objects, which in themselves are not ironic but when brought together there is a contrast that implies a deeper level of meaning. For example, the person who has coffee in the morning with a vitamin pill followed by a cigarette!

Dramatic irony – a feature of drama where the audience is aware of a situation of which other of the characters are ignorant. Shakespeare is a master at exploiting dramatic irony. When King Duncan arrives at Macbeth's castle he praises the place:

This castle has a pleasant seat; the air
Nimbly and sweetly recommends itself
Unto our gentle senses.

The audience is already aware from the scene before that both Macbeth and Lady Macbeth intend to murder him as he sleeps in the castle.

Sarcasm – watch the spelling of this word! Sarcasm is like irony except that it involves ridicule. It still involves stating the opposite of what you mean but in order to ridicule the object of the sarcasm. For example, to exclaim 'Oh! Well done!' to a pupil who is struggling to answer a question is pure sarcasm. Sarcasm, to be effective, has to have a victim and an audience who will laugh at the victim's pain. Cruel!

Satire – the purpose of satire is to hold man's faults up to ridicule in order to amend them. Sometimes an individual is the object of satire, sometimes a social class, sometimes a government, sometimes the entire human race. But the point is that satire, though it uses sarcasm, ridicule, invective, nevertheless has a greater purpose – it is to bring about change. *Gulliver's Travels* by Jonathan Swift is perhaps the most famous example of satire, though some of the cleverer television comedies are satirical in their intent.

Hyperbole (exaggeration) – where the writer deliberately exaggerates for emphatic effect. Again in *Macbeth*, long after the murder, Lady Macbeth sleepwalks and laments:

> *Here's the smell of blood still. All the perfumes of Arabia will not sweeten this little hand.*

Meiosis (understatement) – almost the opposite of hyperbole, where the writer understates the truth for emphasis. Again in *Macbeth*, after the night of the murder, when all kinds of awful things have happened in nature – storms, chimneys blown down, earthquakes – Macbeth comments: *'Twas a rough night.* Too true – he had just murdered the King.

Litotes – statement containing two negatives to emphasise the positive:

> *My not inconsiderable wealth, No Mean City, Not bad!*

Euphemism – the Americans love them! Euphemism is the expression of harsh or unpleasant ideas couched in softer terms. *Passed away* for *died*. *He is a stranger to the truth* for *liar*. *Restroom* for *toilet*.

Periphrasis (circumlocution) – stating something in a roundabout way. Often used for humour or, like euphemism, to avoid harsh ideas or words. *Terminological inexactitude* for *lies*.

Prolepsis – we have met under sentence structure. This device is where the writer anticipates a response (*And before you say…*) or treats something as though it has already happened (*I am dead, Horatio*).

11 Meaning

Meanings of words

Exam examples 1–3

Meanings of ideas

Exam examples 4–6

Questions on both passages

Examples of a question on both passages 1–3

The Close Reading Paper and Textual Analysis – the difference

MEANINGS OF WORDS

In the Close Reading paper, you will be asked about the meaning of words and the meaning of ideas. What is really important to remember is that words don't exist in a vacuum – they exist in a context, and the meaning will depend on or emerge from that context. For example, take the word *stall*. You can consult a dictionary and discover that the word is a noun, meaning a compartment or shed; it is another name for a stable; a small often temporary stand or booth for the display and sale of goods; a row of seats in a church; a pen; an instance of an engine stalling; a condition of an aircraft in flight in which a reduction in speed or an increase in the aircraft's angle causes a sudden loss of lift resulting in a downward plunge; a seat in a theatre or cinema that resembles a chair usually fixed to the floor; the area of seats on the ground floor of a theatre or cinema nearest to the stage or screen.

11 Meaning

There is, then, a huge range of meanings and the actual meaning of the word *stall* in a given sentence will be revealed by the context. For example:

> *The horse was really reluctant to go into its stall.*

The meaning of *stall* in this context is made clear by the use of the word *horse* and the expression *reluctant to go into*.

In the Close Reading paper, the questions about the meanings of words usually ask you (a) to give the meaning, and (b) show how the context helped you arrive at the meaning.

EXAM EXAMPLE 1

Let's turn again to the WIPP passage that we first looked at on page 46. The first sentence of the opening paragraph is reproduced below:

> *Most of all the stuff earmarked for Waste Isolation Pilot Plant (WIPP) in the New Mexico desert is plutonium-contaminated detritus which emits relatively low quantities of radio activity – gloves, bits of drill, flasks, valves, rags, test-tubes, pipes, sludge, shoes, lab coats, and so on.*

The question was:

> **Show how the first sentence provides a context which enables you to understand the meaning of the word 'detritus'.**

> It is important to know that the word *context* refers not only to other words in the sentence but also to features of punctuation which signal meaning.

Obviously, it helps if you know the meaning of the word *detritus*, though many candidates that year did not know what it meant, but those who had been taught how to answer this kind of question were able to arrive at the meaning.

Look at the context:

- *contaminated* provides a bit of a clue that *detritus* in this instance is polluted waste;
- the list – *gloves, bits of drill, flasks, valves, rags, test-tubes, pipes, sludge, shoes, lab coats, and so on* – also suggests disposable waste;

88 *Higher English* **Grade Booster**

- the dash clearly signals to the reader that the list of examples is an explanation of *detritus*.

EXAM EXAMPLE 2

Here is the first paragraph of a recent passage used in the Higher:

> *If you read a wonderful new book by sociologist Frank Furedi – Paranoid Parenting – you will see the story of a teacher who quit the profession after a school trip was cancelled. Some parents were worried the trip would involve their children in a 45-minute journey in a private car. Would the cars be roadworthy? Were the drivers experienced? Were these no-smoking cars?*

The question was:

> **How does the story told in the first paragraph help you to understand the meaning of the word 'paranoid'?** [2 marks]

Note (as always) the number of marks – two marks. Since you are asked to give the meaning of only one word, there will be one mark for meaning and one mark for context.

Answer:

> Paranoid in this context means intense, almost unnecessary, fear or suspicion and clearly the parents' questions at the end of the paragraph make clear their worries about the roadworthiness of the cars, the competence of the drivers, and the possibility of a smoke-filled car interior. These anxieties are referred to as paranoia because they are so over-exaggerated.

Again, you notice that reference is being made to the context – which includes, in this case, sentence structure as well as other word choice.

EXAM EXAMPLE 3

Again from a recent Higher. This, too, is the opening paragraph of the passage from an article by Ruth Wishart:

> *If you hail from Glasgow you will have friends or relatives whose roots lie in the Irish Republic. You will have Jewish friends or colleagues whose grandparents,*

Meaning

> a good number of them Polish or Russian, may have fled persecution in Europe. You will eat in premises run by Italian or French proprietors. It is a diverse cultural heritage enriched now by a large and vibrant Asian population and a smaller but significant Chinese one.

The question was:

> **By referring closely to the first paragraph, show how you are helped to understand the meaning of the expression 'diverse cultural heritage'.** [2 marks]

Since you have to give the meaning of an expression, there will be one mark for showing your understanding of 'diverse' and one mark for showing your understanding of 'cultural heritage'. Although both marks are for demonstrating your understanding of the term, nevertheless you must make reference to the context otherwise you will score only one mark.

The answer:

> *The very varied range of Irish, French, Polish descendents, along with the Asian and Chinese, provides the context that makes clear that 'Diverse cultural heritage' means a set of inherited shared values, customs, and knowledge that is as wide ranging as it is varied.*

MEANINGS OF IDEAS

As well as questions about the meanings of words, you can also be asked about the meaning of ideas. These questions are invariably straightforward to answer since all that is involved is a sensible reading of the passage and an ability to make points in your own words.

EXAM EXAMPLE 4

For example, from the same passage that we examined in example 3 above, comes these two paragraphs:

> *Surely the most sensible way to 'crack down' on illegal workers is to permit legal alternatives. Not just because of woolly liberalism – though that's a perfectly good, decent instinct – but because of enlightened self-interest.*

Meaning

Recently, I was reading an analysis of what was happening to the economy in the Highlands and Islands. The writer welcomes the fact that the population of that area has gone up 20% in a generation. But he goes on to say that 'Labour shortages of every kind are becoming the biggest single constraint in the way of additional economic expansion.' He adds: 'In principle the solution to this problem is readily available in the shape of the so-called asylum seekers or economic migrants that our country, like most countries, seems determined to turn away.'

While, for the most part, immigrants to the Highlands and Islands have recently come from England, the future lies in casting the net much wider. That would be, after all, yet another Scottish solution to a Scottish problem, given that this nation regularly suffers from population loss, exporting tranches of economic migrants all over the world every year. It's been something of a national hobby, which is why there is almost no corner of the globe where you won't stumble over a Caledonian society enthusiastically peopled by folks who will do anything for the old country bar live in it.

The question (slightly adapted) was:

> **Read carefully these two paragraphs. Using your own words as far as possible, outline three important points about immigration that are made in those paragraphs.** [3 marks]

There are, in fact, many points made in these two paragraphs. Any one of these points is worth one mark:

- we should devise legal means of allowing illegal workers to stay;
- this would be in line with our naturally liberal/humane attitudes;
- it would in our economic interests to encourage immigration;
- the Highlands and Islands economy would benefit because the problem of labour shortage would be solved;
- we should encourage immigrants, not just from England, but from all over the world;
- in any case, Scots have emigrated to all parts of the world over the last century.

In these questions about the meaning of ideas, it is perfectly acceptable to list points – as above. But whatever, make sure you use your own words as far as possible. Some words you cannot change – such as the word *immigrant* – but as far as the ideas are concerned, paraphrase (reword) them as much as possible. Lifts (using the actual words of the passage) will earn no marks!

EXAM EXAMPLE 5

The question can be in a slightly different format. For example, let's look again at the Melanie Reid passage about paranoid parenting. Read carefully the following paragraph:

> Teachers are giving up teaching, and youth organisations are dying because they can't find adults prepared to run them. Everywhere good, inspirational people are turning their backs on children because they are terrified of the children and their parents turning on them, accusing them of all manner of wrong-doing. They can no longer operate, they say, in a climate of suspicion and fear.

The question was:

> **Why, according to the writer in this paragraph, are teachers and youth workers 'turning their backs on children'? Use your own words as far as possible.** [2 marks]

As always with Higher Close Reading, the number of marks are a guide – two marks means two points.

If you look carefully at the paragraph, you will see that there are really four points made:

- schools and youth organisations are losing out because qualified people are leaving;
- they are leaving because they are scared of accusations by children and their parents;
- young people are losing the benefits of being motivated by excellent teachers and youth workers;
- they can no longer work under such conditions of fear.

Any two of these points for one mark each. Again, it is perfectly acceptable to list the answers as above.

Or the question can be in this format:

Meaning

EXAM EXAMPLE 6

Read carefully the next paragraph from the Melanie Reid article:

> *I know how they feel. Some years ago, I organised an event for my child's primary school – a running and cycling race along popular, well-used Forestry Commission cycle-tracks. For safety, parents were to be paired with their offspring; we laid on enough insurance and first aid for a B-list royal wedding. Yet the event was almost called off the night before when I received worried calls from parents who had been out to inspect the route. The track was too rough, they said. The risk of children injuring themselves was too great. It was too dangerous to proceed. As it happened, we did go ahead and everyone had a wonderful time. Children glowed with achievement and self-esteem, unaware of the crisis of parental nerve which overshadowed the whole day.*

The question was:

> **How effective do you do you find the personal anecdote in the above paragraph in supporting the writer's point of view in the passage as a whole.** [3 marks]

Now of course that is almost impossible to answer, since you haven't read the whole passage, but what matters is that you know *how* to answer such questions: make sure that you understand fully the point of the anecdote – in this case, that despite the anxieties of parents, the trip was a success – and then go to the rest of the passage and demonstrate *by appropriate close reference* that this key idea supports (or does not support or only partially supports) her arguments elsewhere.

QUESTIONS ON BOTH PASSAGES

Again it is difficult to demonstrate how to answer such questions since you would need to have both passages in front of you in order to show you exactly how to answer such questions, but the following guidelines will help you enormously. Such questions again can be badly done if you don't know the principles of answering them.

Let's have a look at the kind of questions that have been asked in the past.

Meaning

EXAMPLE OF A QUESTION ON BOTH PASSAGES 1

Sometimes you are asked to choose which of the two passages you think gives you the clearer understanding of the topic concerned. A case can always be made for either passage *because there is no right answer*. Whichever passage you prefer, you must nevertheless refer to both passages.

> If, then, the question asks you to make close reference to *the ideas* of both passages and the question is worth 5 marks, then, for full marks, you must demonstrate in your answer:
> - clear references to the central ideas in *both* passages; and
> - an intelligent understanding of the ideas to which you have referred.

Note that such a question asks only about the ideas of the passage and does not demand any references to style or language. Some questions ask only about style, and others ask about both style and ideas. In *all* cases you must always make close reference to *both* passages.

EXAMPLE OF A QUESTION ON BOTH PASSAGES 2

One year, the question was:

> **Which writer's style do you prefer? Justify your view by referring to both passages and to such features as structure, anecdote, symbolism, imagery, word choice.** [5 marks]

Again, a case will be able to be made for either passage, but this time you do not have to refer to ideas. You have to deal with style, which includes all that you have learned about:

- structure (are the sentences formal or informal?);
- anecdote (does the anecdote effectively illustrate the points being made?);
- symbolism (is the symbolism – metonymy – representative of what is being said?);
- imagery (are the images – especially metaphor – appropriate?), word choice (are the expressions illustrative and apt?);

94 *Higher English* **Grade Booster**

- tone (is the tone humorous and effective?) – look out for amusing anecdotes or amusing use of language (irony, sarcasm) or is the tone formal and serious, and if so is that formal, serious tone apt?; and
- punctuation (does the punctuation help to signal appropriate points?)

EXAMPLE OF A QUESTION ON BOTH PASSAGES 3

Recently, one question on both passages asked:

> **Which of the two writers appears to treat the subject matter more effectively? Justify your choice by referring to such features as ideas, tone, use of examples. You should refer to both passages in your answer.** [6 marks]

Again, a case will be able to be made for either passage, but there must be reference to both passages. For full marks you must give evaluative comment. Try to avoid 'I think…', but a useful formula is

> *Although the tone of the first passage is more serious, for example in (give an example of formal, serious tone), nevertheless the ironic humour of the second passage (give an example of irony) makes it easier to understand the writer's point that (state the writer's main point).*

Another good formula is:

> *On the one hand…while on the other hand.*

Or:

> *Not only is x the case concerning the first passage, but y is the case concerning the second passage.*

Meaning

THE CLOSE READING PAPER AND TEXTUAL ANALYSIS – THE DIFFERENCE

Because Close Reading and Textual Analysis have been mentioned in the same sentences, you might be wondering if there is a difference between the two. There is: Close Reading concerns passages which explore an argument or line of thought. The questions, then, will necessarily involve your understanding of the meanings of words within a context and the meanings of ideas within a wider context.

Of course, there will also be questions exploring writer technique – questions which will explore your understanding and appreciation of structure, word choice, imagery, tone, humour, conclusions, anecdotes, and punctuation.

Questions in the Textual Analysis assessment, on the other hand, tend specifically to probe writer technique: questions about narrative stance, point of view, setting, mood/atmosphere/tone, formality, word choice and connotations, punctuation, imagery, literary devices; and for poetry, questions about rhyme, rhythm, **enjambement**, sound.

The kind of questions you will be asked about Textual Analysis, then, is the subject of the next chapter.

12 Textual Analysis

Writing techniques

Writing techniques in poetry

Worked examples 1–2

The Close Reading Paper and Textual Analysis – Conclusion

Textual Analysis assessments tend to present you with writing (poetry, prose, or drama) that explores feelings, attitudes, emotions, reflection, and with questions which are very much about technique – *how* the effects of the writing have been achieved.

WRITING TECHNIQUES

Here are some guidelines to help you with your approach to Textual Analysis:

> It is vitally important to remember that whenever you are presented with a text – short story, novel, play, poem – or even a film or television drama – you have first of all to ask yourself what that text is about. In other words identify theme.

> Thereafter, in attempting to understand and evaluate how the author has portrayed that theme, keep the following techniques in mind. These are the areas about which you are most likely to be questioned:

1 Questions about narrative stance (or voice).

In other words, questions which ask you to analyse how the piece is told or narrated:

(a) first or third person narration – consider the effect (the advantages/disadvantages); occasionally, an author may use second person narration;
(b) if third person narration is used, does the point of view shift or centre on one character – consider the effect;
(c) use of dialogue and its purpose – to establish character, drive forward the narrative.

The following example from *Waiting Room* by Moira Andrew demonstrates the importance of being aware of **narrative voice**. Here are the last two stanzas of the poem:

> *She waits defiantly, fumbling*
> *to light a cigarette, veins*
> *snaking across her hands*
> *like unravelled knitting. A man's face,*
> *preoccupied by youth, looks on.*
>
> *We leave her, the stick a third leg,*
> *waiting to obey the gong,*
> *(Saturday, boiled eggs for tea)*
> *waiting for the rain to stop,*
> *waiting for winter, waiting.*

Note that the narrative stance shifts from third person (where the point of view focuses entirely on the old lady) to first person narration – *We leave her...* Clearly, the *We* is the old lady's family and it is when you notice the switch to first person narration that you realise that the old lady is in a nursing home. Not only that, but the idea of the family leaving her is another method by which the author elicits sympathy for the old lady. Also, recognition of the family's presence is likely to help the reader understand that the photograph in the previous verse is most probably that of her husband, whom we can assume to be dead.

2 Questions about the ways in which setting in place and time are both established – and the effects of both.

For example, look carefully at the first two sentences of George Orwell's *A Hanging*.

> *It was in Burma, a sodden morning of the rains. A sickly light, like yellow tinfoil, was slanting over the high walls into the jail yard.*

Look how in two lines he establishes setting – Burma, in a prison. And time – early morning. We then know that the piece is going to be about a prisoner's execution: the title is *A Hanging* after all. We therefore know that the piece is going to be serious, an effect that is reinforced by *high walls* and *jail yard*, terms that have connotations of restriction and unpleasantness.

3 Questions about how atmosphere/mood/tone is established – use of word choice, connotations of words, weather, physical things.

Again, in the Orwell extract, look how he uses the symbol of the weather. Rain is often used by writers to establish mood: serious, sad, gloomy, depressing. Note how that mood is reinforced by the word *sodden*, which makes the rain almost physical; it is so wet that everything is soaked through. The rain (and all that it represents symbolically) has permeated every aspect of the setting.

But also note the words *sickly* and *yellow tinfoil* and *slanting*, all of which again contribute to the mood. *Sickly* not only suggests decay but also that things are ill, an image supported by his use of *yellow* which also suggests – in this context – illness: when our eyes and skin turn yellow, it is an indication that something is seriously wrong.

Sometimes, however, a tone can be humorous – in which case, look out for irony or sarcasm!

4 Questions about the formality of the writing.

Formality or informality is detected by analysing the sentences – considerable subordination usually makes for a fairly formal piece, whereas short sentences or indeed minor sentences can indicate informality. Look for variety in sentence structure – a long sentence followed by a short one can have a dramatic effect. Many questions can suggest an inquisitorial tone. Understanding formality will help you with questions about tone.

For example, here is an extract from a short story by Edgar Allan Poe. It concerns the discovery of an Egyptian mummy, through whose nose an electric shock had been passed. The effect was instantaneous: the mummy opened its eyes, winked, sneezed, sat up, shook its fist, then addressed its discoverers 'in very capital Egyptian':

> *'I must say, gentlemen, that I am as much surprised as I am mortified at your behaviour. Of Doctor Ponnonner nothing better was to be expected. He is a poor little fat fool who knows no better. I pity and forgive him. But you, Mr Gliddon – who have travelled and resided in Egypt until one might imagine you to the manner born – you, I say, who have been so much among us that you speak Egyptian fully as well, I think, as you write your mother tongue – you,*

12 Textual Analysis

> whom I have always been led to regard as the firm friend of the mummies – I really did anticipate more gentlemanly conduct from you. What am I to think of your standing quietly by and seeing me thus unhandsomely used? What am I to suppose by your permitting Tom, Dick and Harry to strip me of my coffins, and my clothes, in this wretchedly cold climate? In what light (to come to the point) am I to regard your aiding and abetting that miserable little villain, Doctor Ponnonner, in pulling me by the nose?

The language of the above paragraph is formal. Apart from the fact that it is introduced by the phrase 'in very capital Egyptian', the language alone suggests formality. Poe uses expressions such as *I must say, gentlemen* where the *must say* and *gentlemen* are markers of formal English: to address a group of people as *gentlemen* is enough to portray a formal tone. Furthermore, the expression *as much surprised as I am mortified* by its neat complexity is another indication of formality.

The long parenthesis – *who have travelled and resided in Egypt until one might imagine you to the manner born* – is a further marker of formality. (Remember that parenthesis means additional information which is not part of the grammar of the sentence.) Also the expression *until one might imagine you to the manner born* indicates formality with the use of *one* instead of *I*, and the phrase *to the manner born* is not only formal in tone, with the word *born* at the end of the prepositional phrase, but it is also a quotation from Shakespeare – a marker of at least an educated mummy!

But, of course, the whole piece is an extended joke. Part of the humour lies in the fact that this 4000 year-old mummy is perfectly capable of speaking 'capital Egyptian', though we recognise it to be capital English – again part of the humour. It is the very formality of the piece that creates the wit. More humour lies in the use of the word *mortified*, which means *embarrassing* though *in this context* its association with death (mortuary, mortician) is fairly obvious.

But you should also note the subordination. Look at the sentence in the middle of the paragraph:

> But you, Mr Gliddon – who have travelled and resided in Egypt until one might imagine you to the manner born – you, I say, who have been so much among us that you speak Egyptian fully as well, I think, as you write your mother tongue – you, whom I have always been led to regard as the firm friend of the mummies – I really did anticipate more gentlemanly conduct from you.

The very length of the sentence is a marker of formality. The main clause comes at the end of the sentence: *I really did anticipate more gentlemanly conduct from you* and the clauses at the beginning are all subordinate, creating both formality and climax. Interestingly, each of the clauses is introduced by the dash, which helps to clarify each one of them and thus enhance the meaning: the mummy feels betrayed by Mr Gliddon.

5 Questions about word order.

These are usually in the form of a question about sentence structure, the answer to which can be lists (of various kinds) or an alteration of word order. Jill Tweedie, a famous columnist for *The Guardian* once wrote: *every silver lining has its cloud*. Maybe I can leave you to comment on that one!

6 Questions about punctuation and how it is used to support meaning.

It is worth re-reading chapter 8 to ensure you are confident about punctuation.

7 Questions about connotations of words.

As you read the poem, prose extract, or drama extract, be aware of the connotations of words throughout. Also look for the use of symbols used in the piece of writing – weather, seasons, journeys, etc.

The following sentences are from near the beginning of *Dracula* by Bram Stoker. It is the moment when Jonathan Harker first knocks on Count Dracula's door:

> *…I heard a heavy step approaching behind the great door, and saw through the chinks the gleam of a coming light. Then there was the sound of rattling chains and the clanking of massive bolts drawn back. A key was turned with the loud grating noise of long disuse, and the great door swung back.*

> *Within, stood a tall old man, clean shaven save for a long white moustache, and clad in black from head to foot, without a single speck of colour about him anywhere. He held in his hand an antique silver lamp, in which the flame burned without chimney or globe of any kind, throwing long, quivering shadows as it flickered in the draught of the open door.*

The connotations of words such as *heavy step, chinks, rattling chains, clanking of massive bolts, loud grating noise, long disuse, clad in black from head to foot, without a single speck of colour, long, quivering shadows, flickered in the draught* – all create the atmosphere of a horror story. *Rattling* and *clanking* are frightening noises, associated with horror, and, of course *black* has connotations of evil. The Count's colourlessness suggests something unhealthy, while *shadows* permit evil things to lurk, waiting. What is here is not just the description of the Count's castle, but powerful symbols foreshadowing events to come.

8 **Questions about imagery (metaphor, simile, oxymoron and other literary devices, such as alliteration, onomatopoeia) – remember that these devices appear in prose as well as poetry.**

You have to examine the appropriateness of the imagery before being able to comment on its effectiveness. Bear in mind that images are not always visual, but can be to do with hearing, touch, smell, and taste.

Look at the following lines from *Anthem for Doomed Youth* by Wilfred Owen:

> *What passing-bells for these who die as cattle?*
> *Only the monstrous anger of the guns.*
> *Only the stuttering rifles' rapid rattle*
> *Can patter out their hasty orisons.*

The image *die as cattle* conjures up a picture of the way in which animals are killed in a slaughterhouse: in huge numbers, unknowingly, unresistingly, blood everywhere. That seems an apt simile to describe the way in which men died in the trenches of the First World War: they were slaughtered, unknowingly, unresistingly, in huge numbers. But also look at the *stuttering rifles' rapid rattle*: here the use of alliteration not only draws the reader's attention to the meaning of the line but it also captures the very sound of the gunfire with the alliteration of the *r* and the *t* sounds.

WRITING TECHNIQUES IN POETRY

If the Textual Analysis assessment is poetry, you should follow all the points above – they apply equally to poetry, including narrative stance and point of view, though, of course, the poem may not be a narrative one. But techniques specific to poetry are: verse structure, rhyme scheme, **enjambement**, line length, line endings, positioning, rhythm, and sound, which is created by devices such as **alliteration**, **assonance**, **onomatopoeia**, and rhyme.

WORKED EXAMPLE 1

Look at the opening of *The Wasps' Nest* by George MacBeth:

> *All day to the loose tile behind the parapet*
> *The droning bombers fled: in the wet gutter*
> *Belly-upwards the dead were lying, numbed*
> *By October cold. And now the bloat queen,*
> *Sick-orange, with wings draped, and feelers trailing,*

Textual Analysis 12

> *Like Helen combing her hair, posed on the ledge*
> *Twenty feet above the traffic.*

The poet is watching the queen arrive by his window ready to lay her eggs, thus about to create a generation of wasps to be dealt with the following summer. But note the war imagery – *parapet, droning bombers, the dead*. Note also the image of Helen of Troy, whose beauty, it is said, launched a thousand ships and so started the Trojan War – an image which further contributes to the war imagery in the poem. Also, examine the sound: the nasal *n* and *m* sounds of *droning bombers* capture the noise of warplanes and therefore of the wasps themselves. The sound also draws attention to the appropriateness of the image, since bombers and wasps have weapons that can inflict much pain. There is, of course, an element of **hyperbole** here!

There is no rhyme in this poem, but line endings are significant, especially the lines where there is an example of enjambement:

> *Like Helen combing her hair, posed on the ledge*
> *Twenty feet above the traffic.*

The line *Twenty feet above the traffic* spills over from the previous line, but because there is a line ending, there is a pause which makes this line all the more surprising and dramatic.

WORKED EXAMPLE 2

Let's now look at a poem that rhymes. It is by the American poet, Robert Frost:

The Road Not Taken

Two roads diverged in a yellow wood,	a
And sorry I could not travel both	b
And be one traveller, long I stood	a
And looked down one as far as I could	a
To where it bent in the undergrowth;	b

Then took the other, as just as fair,
And having perhaps the better claim,
Because it was grassy and wanted wear;
Though as for that the passing there
Had worn them really about the same,

Textual Analysis

> *And both that morning equally lay*
> *In leaves no step had trodden black.*
> *Oh, I kept the first for another day!*
> *Yet knowing how way leads on to way,*
> *I doubted if I should ever come back.*
>
> *I shall be telling this with a sigh*
> *Somewhere ages and ages hence:*
> *Two roads diverged in a wood, and I –*
> *I took the one less travelled by,*
> *And that has made all the difference.*

The rhyme scheme is quite complex with the first, third and fourth lines rhyming while the second and last line of each verse rhymes. We call this rhyme scheme – a b a a b. It makes the poem seem compact, highly cohesive, which is apt since the thoughts expressed are complex, compact and subtle. The subtlety of the poem is supported by the subtlety of the rhyme, where words such as *both* and *undergrowth* are rhymed: you have to look carefully to notice the rhyme. The poet (or rather the persona – the person narrating the poem) is faced with a decision in life and does not know what path to take. Why a *yellow wood*? In this context *yellow* could mean that the persona is in the autumn of his life or it could be that the colour *yellow* in this context suggests a contemplative tone.

There are examples of **enjambement** in this poem – in this case, run-on verses. Verse two spills over from verse one as does verse three from the second verse. Again this contributes to the compact, cohesive feel to this poem.

The last line is also significant: *And that has made all the difference.* It has the rhythm of everyday speech; indeed, it is almost colloquial, which is what draws attention to the meaning.

Note that in these two examples we analysed what the text is about – you have to do that in order to make sense of the techniques.

> Remember that all texts concern themes – what is the text about? All techniques help reveal/portray/explore the themes.

THE CLOSE READING PAPER AND TEXTUAL ANALYSIS – CONCLUSION

Although these chapters have been about Close Reading and Textual Analysis, you must bear in mind that some of the techniques we have so far looked at will also apply to the Critical Essay, the subject of the next chapter. Indeed, the whole textual analysis approach is one that you should be adopting to the literature that you study – theme, effect and the techniques by which the effects have been achieved. Therefore you need to be sure that you are thoroughly acquainted with all the techniques that we have covered.

13 The Critical Essay – Narrative Structure

Narrative structure

Worked example

Theme

Prose question 1 – Exam example

Prose question 2

The Critical Essay paper involves two essays from more than one **genre**. Genre is a word we use to classify literature. There are three genres of literature: drama, prose and poetry. The Higher Critical Essay paper has five sections:

- Section A – Drama;
- Section B – Prose;
- Section C – Poetry;
- Section D – Mass Media; and
- Section E – Language.

We will concern ourselves with the first three of those sections.

But first of all a word about literature. Although the most obvious purpose of language is to communicate, it is not its only purpose. For example, when you meet a friend and ask: *How are you?* do you really want an answer? The question looks and is framed as though you are enquiring after the friend's health, physical, mental, or emotional, or all three, but you aren't. The last thing you expect is a detailed medical report! You are merely greeting the person in a polite and socially acceptable way. The language has more to do with your attitudes and feelings than it has to do with communication. The language of literature is a bit like that – it has a great deal to do with feelings and emotions.

The purpose of this book, however, is not so much to teach you how to study literature but to teach you how to answer the Critical Essay paper. Before we launch into that, however, let us look at narrative structure. Most of you will study a novel and/or a short story; some of you may even tackle the non-fiction question. Whenever it comes to prose, however, you need to know about narrative structure.

NARRATIVE STRUCTURE

All art, by definition, is artificial – it is created by someone who takes very conscious decisions about how the finished product will appear: a painting, a pop song, a play, a novel, a short story, or a poem. If it has been artificially produced then we, as critics, can examine – analyse – how the piece has been put together. This process is sometimes referred to as **deconstruction**.

When it comes to literature, perhaps the most important lesson to learn is that an author, probably before beginning to write, takes decisions about setting, characterisation, **plot**, dialogue, etc. To explain: let's suppose that you want to make a film which has as its theme the eeriness of the supernatural. To begin with, you might decide to use black-and-white – your first conscious decision about a technique that will contribute to your chosen theme. You might then decide to set it in a large, remote house with a long isolated driveway that wends its way through trees and undergrowth. You also decide to set it at night, where the dark setting adds to the eeriness. You choose two characters – a vulnerable, middle-aged woman and her disabled son… her husband died violently in a car crash the summer before.

You get the idea? When we come to criticise – analyse (or deconstruct) your work – we can, then, examine how it has been put together. That is the work of the literary critic.

It is also really important that you grasp the difference between author and narrator. The author is the person who sits at the word processor taking decisions about setting, characterisation, plot, atmosphere. The author also takes decisions about *who* will tell the story – a narrator or a character in the novel itself. When the novel/short story is being told in the third person, the person telling the story is the *narrator* (or *narrative voice*), not to be confused with the author.

But a word of warning here: although we examine, criticise, analyse, deconstruct, evaluate *how* an author has put the novel, play, or poem together, the one area we need to enter with care is *why* he or she put it together. Often you will hear people talk about the author's purpose – be careful because such talk can be dangerous: it leads you into the realms of psychology and not criticism. We do not know *why* Shakespeare wrote *Romeo and Juliet* or *why* he had Romeo kill himself at the end; we can only analyse the effect of his decisions.

Discussion of author purpose, however, is more useful when we are examining non-fiction: the purpose behind a telephone directory or newspaper article on politics or the ethics of scientific experimentation is much clearer than the purpose behind Arthur Miller's *Death of a Salesman*.

But let's get back to narrative structure. Narrative structure is the overall structure of a story. Usually, the author decides to make the structure chronological – the events are told in time sequence: beginning, middle, and end, though sometimes the author chooses to relate it in a middle, beginning, and end sequence (i.e. **flashback**).

An author can choose to tell a story in four main ways – see below.

1   Omniscient narrator

The story is told by a narrator (who has been created by the author); the narrator knows everything about all the characters. The author puts the narrator in the position of knowing everything – about what characters say, hear, see, feel, taste, smell. But more than that: this narrator knows their most intimate thoughts and motivations better than they do themselves simply because the omniscient narrator tells us everything.

2   First person narration

The story is told by one of the characters. The advantage of this method of narration is that the reader gets to know the character intimately, but the disadvantage is that the character telling the story has to be present at all times. The reader's information is filtered through the mind of the character narrating the story. The result of all this of course is that we cannot know the intimate thoughts of the other characters because the narrator (being a character in the novel and not omniscient) cannot know them.

Sometimes, however, there is multiple narration, where more than one character tells the story: the most classic example of multiple narration is *Dracula* by Bram Stoker where there are several narrators – Jonathan Harker, Dr Seward, Van Helsing, Mina Harker, and Lucy Westenra, each of whom uses a different method of narrating the story. *Wuthering Heights* by Emily Brontë has two narrators – Lockwood and Nellie Dean.

3   Third person narration

Similar to omniscient narrator except that the narrator focuses only on one character and all events are seen through that character's eyes. The story is told in the third person but, since the narrator focuses on a particular character, that character has to be present at all times. Many short stories are told in third person narration, where the **point of view** is restricted to one character.

4   Stream of consciousness

The narrative is structured in a much less conventional way than first person narration. The writer tries to capture, in a stream of consciousness novel, the natural, normal thinking processes of an actual human being; thus in the narrative the reader is faced with the character's distractions, daydreams, memories, and other thoughts triggered by what he/she has seen, or is thinking about, or by a word that he/she has just used. You should have a look at the work of Virginia Woolf and you will see what I mean.

Stream of Consciousness is very much a 20th century development in the novel.

5   Second person narration

Sometimes part of the narrative is told in the second person – the *you* form – which creates an intimate immediate relationship with the character telling the story. The most obvious example of this form is in *Complicity* by Ian Banks, where the murderer narrates his murders in second person.

These 'ways' are sometimes referred to as the **point of view** – and, remember, you have point of view in poems as well as in prose. Sometimes, especially within a poem, the point of view shifts, though this can be the case in a novel as well. Short stories are often told in third person narration, though the point of view can shift.

A WORKED EXAMPLE

Let's look at an example of point of view shifting. Remember we looked at an extract from the short story *Heart Songs* by E. Annie Proulx? Let's look at some more of it:

> Catherine sat in the tan recliner. Her eyes were closed and the desolate fluttering blue light mottled her tired face and the white shirt printed with the dancing dog and the word Poochie's Grill. Snipe turned off the lurching images and she opened her pale eyes. She was thin, a mayonnaise blonde with very light blue eyes like transparent marbles. Surly, ugly, she had a flat rump

13   The Critical Essay – Narrative Structure

AND BEAUTIFUL STRONG LEGS WITH SWELLING CALVES. <u>She was also getting tired of being broke, getting close to sniffing out Snipe's longing for a gutter.</u>

<u>'You got a job, I hope,' she said.</u>

'Ahhh,' said Snipe, GRINNING LIKE A SET OF TEETH ON A DISH, 'there really wasn't any job after all. We just played. But some very fine country stuff.' He tried to pump some of the old, boy-genius enthusiasm into his voice, to imitate the confident manner he'd used with Catherine two years before when they sat up until three in the morning drinking expensive wine she had bought and making plans for living by selling bundles of white birch logs tied with red ribbon to fireplace owners in New York City, or growing ginseng roots they would sell through a friend whose brother knew a pharmacist in Singapore. 'Cath, this is an undiscovered group and there's money there, big bucks – records, promotions, tours. The works. This could be the one, baby, it's the one that could get us on the way.' He couldn't keep the secret revulsion at the thought of success out of his voice. At once she was furious and shouting.

'My God, no job! Gas and money wasted. I work my butt off down in that kitchen' – she plucked at her Poochie's Grill shirt with disgust – 'while you bum around playing free music. The rent on this place with its dismal rotten trees is coming up next week, and I haven't got it, and I'm not borrowing it from my parents again. It's your turn, buddy. Rob a bank if you have to, but you pay the rent!'

SNIPE KNEW SHE WOULD GET THE MONEY FROM HER PARENTS. 'WHAT'S SO GODDAM TOUGH ABOUT MAKING A FEW HAMBURGERS TO KEEP THE SHIP FLOATING?' HE SAID. 'I'VE GOT TO BUILD UP MY MUSICAL CONTACTS HERE BEFORE I CAN EXPECT TO MAKE ANY MONEY. IT TAKES TIME, ESPECIALLY IN THE COUNTRY. IT'S MORE IMPORTANT I'M DOING SOMETHING I REALLY LIKE, YOU KNOW THAT.' HE COULDN'T SAY TO HER THAT WHAT HE LIKED WAS THE FAILING KITCHEN CHAIR, THE WRECKED PICK-UP IN THE WEEDS.

Look carefully at how the point of view shifts between Catherine and Snipe: I have used underlining to indicate Catherine's point of view, small capital letters to indicate Snipe's and full-sized capital letters to indicate what might be the narrator's point of view. Now these are my suggestions: remember there is no right answer – you can disagree.

> Note that Catherine's 'question' – 'You got a job, I hope,' she said – although in the language of a question, nevertheless has no question mark, which clearly indicates that her tone is not one of concerned enquiry but of unsympathetic expectation that Snipe has indeed got a job. Interesting use (or absence) of punctuation, which the sensitive reader should note.

110   *Higher English* **Grade Booster**

THEME

The critical reader should be aware of various aspects of the novel. Perhaps the most important aspect of the novel (or of any work of literature) is the theme. All the techniques are there to reveal, explore, portray the theme.

The theme of a work of fiction is what it is about, its central concerns, its ideas. Any novel or short story will explore some issue, usually of significance to the human situation, condition, or experience. The writer has to establish this issue or theme by means of the setting, the characterisation and the plot, in other words by the various techniques listed below.

There are, then, a number of techniques by which the theme is portrayed or revealed or explored:

1 Characterisation

The writer must establish the major characters for the story. Clearly, these characters will be developed by their interaction with each other, with the setting, and with the plot. An author can use a variety of techniques to build up character: by the use of dialogue, the actions of the character, the reactions of others, the language used by the narrator.

The writer must also establish the minor characters who will be used for a variety of effects. It is vitally important to see all characters as a product of the writer's imagination and technical skill and *not* as having a life of their own independent of the work of fiction. A *character study* can be a misleading term since it suggests that the character being studied has a life outside the work of fiction; a character study should avoid psychoanalysis and concentrate on literary technique.

2 Setting

The writer must also establish an appropriate setting, both in time and place.

> Too often, we forget that time is as vital an aspect of setting as place.

Not only should we be concerned with the time in which the novel is set and the time span which it covers, but also we should pay attention to when it was written since that is a dimension of time that will affect what the novel is about.

3 Plot

A series of incidents does not constitute plot. Plot must always involve causality – one incident is caused by another. Thus, the famous example: *The king died and then the queen died* is a series of incidents but not plot, whereas *The king died and then the queen died of grief* is plot. Plot will always be in a chronological sequence – *beginning > middle > end* – though sometimes we can have *middle > beginning > end*, sometimes (as noted already) referred to as **flashback**.

4 Symbolism

An author often uses symbols to represent the ideas or characters or tone in the novel. The study of signs or symbols is called **semiotics** – an important technique in the novel or in any art form. Symbols can involve anything from the use of weather to the use of colour and flowers. The sea, forests, mountains, deserts can all be used as powerful **signifiers**, as can the use of period costume, urban scenes, trams, cars, trains.

5 Atmosphere/mood/tone

Right at the very beginning of the novel the writer has to establish an appropriate atmosphere or mood or tone which enhances and supports the ideas. This can be done by means of word choice, imagery, symbolism or a combination of all three.

One can see authors as highly manipulative people who take delight in controlling people and situations and can use the above techniques greatly to their advantage. Authors move characters about as though on a chess board though, unlike chess players, they are free to set the game anywhere they choose and can change the rules as they go along. One should not, however, confuse one's ability to decipher the results of this manipulation with a desire to probe the author's motives – that should be left for the psychologists. All talk of author purpose or author intention should be avoided, yet one should be able to work out the effects of some of the author's artistic or literary decisions. The author, then, is the person behind it all, the person who creates the narrator or 'narrative voice' of the story: all stories, including a text book – including **this** text book – have a narrative voice.

The Critical Essay – Narrative Structure

A word about structure and style. The distinction between structure and style is not easy to define. It is easier when you think in concrete terms: a room has structure – its measurements, its overall shape, what the materials are from which it is made. Its style is really how it has been decorated – colour of the walls, kind of furniture, modern, Art Deco, minimalist, etc. It is the same with literature – the structure is the overall structure of the piece – beginning, middle, end, fiction, non-fiction, reflective, analytical – whereas the style is the way in which it has been written – imagery, humour, sentence-structure, dialogue, etc.

A final word about theme and meaning: the theme has to do with the *meaning* of a text, but meaning, we have established, has nothing to do with what the author intends. So what **has** meaning to do with?

> Meaning emerges from the relationship between the text and the reader, but the reader has to be aware that the context will impose its own constraints on that meaning.

And that is important: it is up to the reader to imagine the meanings of a text, but the text itself will impose its own constraints on the range of meanings. We discovered that when we first examined connotations on page 67. Whatever you claim to be the meaning of a text, you need to support that claim by reference to the text.

It is important to bear all of this in mind when you are analysing a text, either for your Personal Study or in preparation for the Critical Essays in the examination itself. All texts deal with issues or themes, but, since each reader is different – in experience and personality – then each interpretation of that text will also be different. But whatever meaning you derive from the text, you have to be able to justify your ideas by reference to the text. Back to the *Romeo and Juliet* example: however you read that text – whether it is about teenage sex, or about the inability of pure, romantic love to survive the enduring hatred among human beings, or about the role of fate in our lives – what really matters is that you can justify your view by giving detailed examples from the text to support your opinion.

If you look at the kind of questions that are asked in the prose section, you will see that the above information is not only important but essential.

13 The Critical Essay – Narrative Structure

PROSE QUESTION 1 – EXAM EXAMPLE

This is from a very recent Higher Critical Analysis paper:

> Choose *a novel* in which your admiration for a particular character grows as the plot unfolds.
> Explain briefly why your admiration increases and, in more detail, discuss how the writer achieves this.
> In your answer you must refer closely to the text and to at least *two* of: characterisation, theme, key incidents, structure, or any other appropriate feature.

Note that you have to do two things: explain briefly why your admiration for a particular character increases **and** discuss the techniques by which the writer achieves the effect of increasing your admiration for the character. Right away you see that you have to deal with techniques. You are given a list of techniques (with the exception of theme, which, as I have pointed out already, is not a technique).

Which two techniques from the list should we choose? You cannot answer a question on character without dealing with character, therefore that is one of the techniques we need to deal with. The other probably depends on the novel, but it is likely that there would be some key scene or incident which causes your admiration to increase. To answer the question, you need to deal with characterisation and key scene or incident, probably including point of view. If setting is relevant to your answer them maybe setting should be considered rather than key scene.

> The interaction between character and setting is often a vital aspect of a novel in revealing or developing theme.

PROSE QUESTION 2

> Choose a novel which you enjoyed because of the effectiveness of the ending.
> Explain how the ending satisfies you and adds to your appreciation of the novel.
> In your answer you must refer closely to the text and to at least two of: climax, theme, characterisation, plot, or any other appropriate feature.

Once again, you are asked to do two things: explain the ways in which the ending satisfies you **and** to say how that adds to your appreciation of the novel. In this case, you cannot really avoid dealing with characterisation and theme because of the way in which the theme is resolved by the ending. It could be that what appealed to you was the build-up to the climax, in which case you need to deal with the suspense, as an aspect of plot, created by the author.

Although nearly every question refers to '*your* appreciation' or '*your* interest' or 'what *you* found convincing', you should try to avoid introducing yourself into your answer. The examiners use the word *you* and *your* in the questions as a way of getting you – the candidate – involved, but it is a bit naïve and unsophisticated to bring yourself into it. Try to avoid the construction:

> *A novel I have read and which captured my interest because of the setting...*

Even worse is when the candidate begins:

> *I am going to write about 'Stone Cold' and I am going to show why I found the ending convincing.*

Much better, as you will see, is to refer to the reader's response and reactions.

Try always to begin your Critical Essay – or the Personal Study – with a formula whereby you:

- mention the author
- mention the title, putting the title into inverted commas

The Critical Essay – Narrative Structure

- use the words of the question to establish relevance
- refer to the reader rather than to yourself.

For example, if you want to use Pat Barker's 'Regeneration' in your answer to the Prose Question 1 above, you could begin:

> *In 'Regeneration' by Pat Barker, the reader's attitude to one of the main characters, Prior, changes as the novel progresses. To begin with, Prior seems...*

Now let's tackle the Personal Study and Critical Essay in more detail.

14 Personal Study and Critical Essays – *What you have to do*

Preparing for assessment

Exam example

PREPARING FOR ASSESSMENT

There are three ways in which your appreciation of literature is assessed throughout your Higher course: Textual Analysis and the Personal Study (both internal assessments) and the Critical Essay (part of the external examination). The Personal Study is just a Critical Essay – but longer: say, 850–1000 words instead of 650–700. We shall concentrate on the Critical Essay, but keep remembering that the Personal Study should be tackled along the same lines.

The Critical Essay forms a vital part of the assessment in your Higher English course. In the Critical Essay paper, there are three literature sections: Drama, Prose and Poetry. There are two other sections – Media Studies and Language – but you must ignore these sections if you have not been taught the relevant courses. You have to choose *two* questions from more than one section, and you have 45 minutes in which to answer each question.

In preparing for this paper you should study a piece (or pieces) of literature from *at least two* of the three genres: a play and/or a prose work and/or some poetry. Ideally, you should prepare for all three sections. Remember that prose work includes fiction (novels, short stories) as well as non-fiction (journalism, essays, autobiography, biography, travel writing).

14 Personal Study and Critical Essays – What you have to do

When preparing for the examination, you need to ask yourself of the texts you are studying the following three questions:

- What is the text about? In other words, what are the themes of the text.
- What effect does it have on me? What reactions do you have to the text?
- How have the effects been achieved? In other words, the literary and linguistic writer techniques.

> Your answer to the first question will provide you with the theme of the text, the answer to the second question will provide you with the effects of the text and your reaction to them, and the answer to the third question will provide you with the ways in which the techniques portray the theme(s) and how the techniques have been achieved (and will, in addition provide you with training for the Textual Analysis section).

It is important that you study and prepare for the examination according to the method outlined above. You need to know the text thoroughly and be able to refer to it, you need to know the techniques used and be able to analyse them, you need to be able to say in what ways these techniques are effective – in other words, you need, for example, to be able to identify alliteration **and** to be able to say that it is effective because it draws attention to meaning and captures the sounds that are appropriate.

You are expected to produce an essay of not less than 650 words in length in response to a question or task, which is very specific.

There are four areas in which you must, in your answer, demonstrate knowledge and skill, especially if you are aiming at a good grade:

(a) Understanding   You must demonstrate thorough knowledge of and insight into the ideas or central concerns of the text **and** you must provide a well-structured response to the demands of the question. You will be able to refer to the text to support your comments.

(b) Analysis   You must demonstrate an analysis of the writer's literary and linguistic techniques. You will be able to refer to the text to support your comments.

(c) Evaluation   You must show that you are engaged with the text (but avoid making empty comments such as 'I really enjoyed *Lord of the Flies*') and show that you are able to evaluate the effectiveness of the techniques and the text as a whole.

118 *Higher English* **Grade Booster**

Personal Study and Critical Essays – What you have to do **14**

You will be able to refer to the text to support your comments.

(d) Expression Spelling, grammar and punctuation will be accurate. Language will be controlled and fluent and you will use appropriate critical terminology (such as metaphor, oxymoron, structure – see the list of Literary Devices, chapter 10) in your analysis.

It is vitally important that you look carefully at the question and determine exactly what is being asked of you. There will be two aspects to the question both of which must be dealt with in your answer.

EXAM EXAMPLE

The following question appeared recently in the Critical Essay paper:

> **Choose a poem about old age.**
> **Explain what impression the poet creates of old age and discuss how effectively the impression is created.**
> **In your answer you must refer closely to the text and to at least two of: theme, structure, word choice, imagery, or any other appropriate feature.**

Look at what you have to do – select a relevant poem, and by referring to, say, word choice and imagery you have to:

- show how the poet creates the impression of old age; and
- discuss how effectively the impression is created.

Let's go through the stages of producing an answer:

(a) You choose to write about *Waiting Room* by Moira Andrew. Here is the poem:

Waiting Room

She waits neatly, bone-china thin,
in a room tight with memories,
claustrophobic with possessions,
rendered down from eighty years,
5 *eight Homes and Garden rooms.*

Higher English **Grade Booster** 119

14 Personal Study and Critical Essays – What you have to do

> *She waits graciously, bearing*
> *the graffiti of age. She drizzles*
> *sherry into fine glasses, tea*
> *into what is left*
> **10** *of wide-brimmed wedding china.*
>
> *With the top of her mind*
> *she is eager to skim off news*
> *of the family, who married whom*
> *and when. Names elude her. Tormented,*
> **15** *she tries to trap them on her tongue.*
>
> *She waits defiantly, fumbling*
> *to light a cigarette, veins*
> *snaking across her hands*
> *like unravelled knitting. A man's face,*
> **20** *preoccupied by youth, looks on.*
>
> *We leave her, the stick a third leg,*
> *waiting to obey the gong,*
> *(Saturday, boiled eggs for tea)*
> *waiting for the rain to stop,*
> **25** *waiting for winter, waiting.*
>
> MOIRA ANDREW

(b) Plan your answer carefully so that you cover all that has been asked of you and you remain relevant. You know that you want to talk about structure, word choice, imagery, and linguistic features, such as sentence structure.

(c) Begin your answer with the words of the question to establish relevance.

> *In 'Waiting Room' by Moira Andrew, the poet has created, by a number of poetic and linguistic techniques, such a powerfully sad impression of old age that the sympathy of the reader is easily engaged.*

(d) Next make clear that you are going to deal with structure, word choice, imagery, and linguistic features – but try not to write 'I'm going to deal with...': in an English literature answer that sounds too mechanistic and unsophisticated. You should write something along the following lines:

> *Moira Andrew portrays the theme of old age and creates the effects of sympathy and sadness by means of a number of techniques such as structure, word choice, imagery, and her deployment of linguistic features.*

120 *Higher English* **Grade Booster**

Personal Study and Critical Essays – What you have to do

(e) Now you need to take each of these techniques and deal with them in turn. But remember that you have decided that the impression of old age created is one of sympathy and sadness, therefore you must keep referring to that impression. Take structure:

> The poem is structured in five verses, each five lines in length. There is no rhyme scheme, nor is the rhythm regular, thus creating a sound very like prose. Such a structure helps reinforce the reflective, rather sad mood of the poem. The first four verses, with the exception of verse three, begin with the words 'She waited...' thus drawing attention to the fact that the old lady now spends her days waiting. The first stanza states that 'She waited neatly', a comment on her appearance, whereas the second stanza begins with 'She waited graciously', drawing attention more to her demeanour and character, thus helping to engage the sympathy of the reader. In the fourth stanza, the words 'She waits defiantly' introduce the idea that this old lady, more than eighty years of age, nevertheless has a strength of character and resilience to be admired, thus further engaging the reader's sympathy.
>
> By the last verse, however, the writer....

And you would go on and talk about the contribution the structure of the last stanza makes to the theme of old age – and the reader's sympathy – by means of the repetition of 'waiting' throughout.

Note also how the point of view shifts in the last stanza: in the previous stanza it has been omniscient narrator but in the final stanza the point of view shifts to the family by means of first person narration – **We leave her...** a technique that also brings sympathy for the old lady since the family that she adores is about to go.

But also note how the quotations have been worked into the sentence structure. Try to avoid the formula of *quotation + comment*. Some candidates write:

> 'She waits defiantly'. This shows that she is a determined lady.

Such a formula lacks sophistication and depth, whereas

> In the fourth stanza, the words 'She waits defiantly' introduce the idea that this old lady, more than eighty years of age nevertheless has a strength of character and resilience to be admired, thus further engaging the reader's sympathy.

indicates a candidate who understands fully how to produce a Critical Essay: to write this way will improve your grade.

(f) Thereafter, take each of the other techniques in turn – word choice, imagery, and linguistic features – and provide three or four paragraphs on each, demonstrating by reference to the text how each contributes to the theme of old age and how each engages the reader's sympathy. Let's take, as an example of linguistic features, a line from the third verse:

> Moira Andrew is able to combine the poetic devices of alliteration and enjambement with her use of sentence structure in order to elicit sympathy for the old lady. For example, in the lines:
>
> > Tormented,
> > She tries to trap them on her tongue.
>
> by placing the word 'Tormented' at the beginning of the sentence (though at the end of the line), thereby breaking the normal word order, she draws attention to the word and its meaning. The old lady is tortured by the fact that she cannot quite remember names of her family, thus making the reader feel sorry for her. The alliteration of the 't' and 'tr' sounds captures the stuttering difficulty the old lady has in remembering the relatives' names. Moreover, this longer sentence is preceded by a short one, thus building up to the idea of the frustration of forgetfulness.

(g) Finally, you have to draw your essay to a conclusion. Signal clearly to the marker that you are summing up:

> Thus it can be seen that by her use of structure, word choice, imagery, and linguistic features, Moira Andrew is able not only to create a powerful image of old age but also to engage the reader's sympathy for the plight of the old lady in the nursing home.

Personal Study and Critical Essays – What you have to do

> The principles for writing a Critical Essay (and the Personal Study) on any other genre are the same: you have to follow the guidelines set out above if you want as high a grade as possible.

But your essay must also be written in accurate and controlled English, spelled correctly, and you must demonstrate your ability to use technical terminology. We shall look at what is expected in the next chapter.

15 Personal Study and Critical Essays – *The importance of accuracy*

- The Critical Essay and Personal Study
- How to set out your Critical Essay
- How to set out your answer
- How to use quotations 1–2
- The conclusion to your essay
- Check your essay

THE CRITICAL ESSAY AND PERSONAL STUDY

While the previous chapter was concerned with *how* to compose a Critical Essay (and, at the same time, a Personal Study) answer, you also need advice about the formality of English that is required. Guidelines for your written Expression are set out on page 119:

(d) Expression   Spelling, grammar and punctuation will be accurate. Language will be controlled and fluent and you will use appropriate critical terminology (such as metaphor, oxymoron, structure – see the list of Literary Devices, chapter 10) in your analysis.

It is, therefore, important, if you want to ensure a top grade, that you consider the following advice about the accuracy of your writing.

HOW TO SET OUT YOUR CRITICAL ESSAY

The person who marks your Critical Essay paper next May will have in the region of 200 to 250 other scripts as well as yours to consider. You should therefore make that person's job as easy as possible by setting out your answer neatly and clearly. The last thing you want to do is irritate your marker because

Personal Study and Critical Essays – The importance of accuracy

of sloppy, careless and unclear work.

You should:

- number your answer (in the margin) to correspond with the question number in the Paper;
- **introduce your material effectively and concisely USING THE WORDING OF THE QUESTION** so that the marker/examiner knows instantly and unambiguously that you know what you are doing;
- ensure that you put the names of titles of prose works, plays and poems into inverted commas;
- ensure that proper names – such as titles, characters and the author's name – begin with a capital letter;
- avoid all informalities, such as abbreviations and/or contractions: do not write *isn't, wasn't, doesn't, can't, shan't*. Write each of these words out in full.

These things may seem all too obvious but it is amazing how many candidates fail to number the answer correctly (causing the marker some grief) and also how many do not begin with the words of the question raising instantly the problem of relevance. No matter how clever and insightful your answer, if you are irrelevant, you will fail.

HOW TO SET OUT YOUR ANSWER

For a top grade, it is vital that you produce a well-composed, well-written and well-structured essay that is relevant, perceptive and coherent. You need to be able to communicate clearly and show detailed understanding of the ways in which the various literary and linguistic techniques create effect and shape meaning. In order to produce all that, you must:

- **plan you answer** – take five minutes to set out the material which you think is relevant to the answer;
- **then, as part of that plan, structure your material appropriately** – ensuring that your answer will cover all aspects of the question asked – see chapter 14;
- **produce a coherent piece of prose** – 'coherent' means that it must make sense by itself because it has been appropriately introduced and concluded;

- **make sure that paragraphs are linked to create cohesiveness;** 'cohesive' means that your essay has to be well-linked and 'hangs together' as a continuous piece of formal prose with a clearly identifiable line of thought or argument running through it. To achieve that end make sure that one paragraph follows logically from the previous by using linking sentences and linking words;
- **make sure that your ideas are also linked and balanced** – use terms such as:

moreover, furthermore, accordingly	Words which give the effect of linkage and development of your argument or line of thought
however, nevertheless	Words which introduce a contrasting idea or ideas
on the one hand x is the case… but on the other y is also the case	An expression which conveys two contrasting ideas that are clearly linked – gives the impression of presenting a balanced argument
not only… but also	An expression which conveys the notion that one idea follows on from the first and develops it – suggests balance
although x is the case, y also is the case	An expression conveying the notion that though two ideas might be contrasting, nevertheless they are clearly connected
therefore, thus, clearly	Words which introduce a conclusion to your argument or line of thought
whereas	A word which introduces a contrasting idea

The importance of relevance:

> Ensure that you establish relevance to the question asked – make sure that you use the words of the question in your first paragraph.

In *Hamlet*, by William Shakespeare, there is a scene of intense emotion which is brought about by the dramatist's use of characterisation, confrontation, and effective dialogue.

When you think about it, how can you discuss drama without discussing characterisation? That thought should help in your preparations!

> Ensure that you keep relevant throughout – make sure that you use the words of the question or at least refer to the question in every paragraph.

Use words such as *since, thus, hence, clearly, similarly* at the beginning of a paragraph – and throughout. These words help to keep you relevant and to develop your line of thought or argument;

HOW TO USE QUOTATIONS 1

Teachers are frequently asked about quotations.

> Please note that the word to use is **quotation** and NOT **quotes**!

The most frequently asked question is: *How many quotations should I learn?* There is no answer to this question since quotations have to be relevant to the question asked and there is no knowing what that will be!

> The best way to prepare for the examination is:
> - to know the themes of the texts that you are studying;
> - to know the techniques by which these themes are portrayed; and
> - to be able to support your ideas about themes and techniques by being able to make close reference to the text.

You should use quotations, then, to support your answers, but you do not really have to be able to quote fully – as long as you can refer to the text to support your argument.

HOW TO USE QUOTATIONS 2

In your answer, try to avoid the formula: *quotation + comment* – e.g. avoid writing: *The author says 'she waited neatly'. This shows that she was neat in appearance.* The formula leads you to make empty comment, or, at best, to give the meaning of the expression you have quoted. Above all, avoid the formula: *quotation, this shows that...* where you use the **comma splice** (see pages 56 and 57)!

> Work all quotations into the very structure of your sentence – for example:
> The first stanza of *Waiting Room* states that 'She waited neatly', a comment on her smart and precise appearance, her clothes and outward attitude, whereas the second stanza begins with 'She waited graciously', drawing attention more to her demeanour and character, thus helping to engage the sympathy of the reader.

THE CONCLUSION TO YOUR ESSAY

It is very important to conclude your essay effectively. After all, it is at the end of your essay that the marker will put the mark, therefore it is to your advantage to have a good summation of your argument.

You should:

- **conclude appropriately** – *Thus…* or *Clearly, it can be seen that…* or even *In conclusion*, and then refer back to the words of the question. Make the conclusion short *and don't introduce any new material*.

CHECK YOUR ESSAY

All of us, even the best of writers, make mistakes in written English, therefore it is important to check your work once you have finished. If you have made a mistake, do not paste the error thick with Tipp-Ex. Simply, put brackets round the error, put one line through the mistake, then insert the correct version above. The marker should be able to see the correction so that he or she can note that you are a conscious writer, capable of improving your work.

Therefore:

- **read carefully what you have written and make corrections** – this is a very important part of the exercise since you will pick up poor linkage, any informalities in style or any of the other *don'ts* listed above!

16 Your Own Writing

The internal assessment
Linguistic and literary devices
The various types of writing

THE INTERNAL ASSESSMENT

As you know, the assessment requirements mean that you have to produce, under supervised conditions, a piece of writing of your own choice, a minimum of 650 words in length. You may, of course, draft the piece beforehand, but you are only permitted notes when producing the piece under supervised conditions. As with the other internal assessments, you only have to pass this exercise: your writing does not have to be graded.

You are able to choose from the following writing types:

- Personal/reflective writing
- Discursive writing
- Creative/imaginative writing
- Persuasive writing

Before we look at each of these kinds of writing, it is important to recall what you have learned throughout this book: reading and writing are incredibly closely related. The more you develop your reading skills and recognise the various linguistic and literary devices, the more you will be able to incorporate these same devices into your own writing. Moreover, your writing also improves because you have absorbed at a subconscious, subliminal level many of the techniques used by skilled writers. You absorb aspects of their imagery, rhythm, sentence structure – and your writing improves as a result.

LINGUISTIC AND LITERARY DEVICES

Let's have a look at some of the linguistic and literary devices that we have already studied for reading purposes and apply them now to your own writing.

Word order

Remember to apply all that you now know about word order. Altering the word order of your sentences not only changes meaning by altering emphasis, it also gives variety to your sentence structure. A good example of the effective alteration of word order is when you place a prepositional phrase at the beginning of a sentence. Let's alter the following sentence:

> *The prisoner was released on the fourth of July as the sun broke through the clouds.*

There are two prepositional phrases in that sentence: *on the fourth of July* and *as the sun broke through the clouds*. Let's try altering the positioning of the prepositional phrases:

> *As the sun broke through the clouds on the fourth of July, the prisoner was released.*

Or even:

> *On the fourth of July, as the sun broke through the clouds, the prisoner was released.*

In the first case, the weather and date are being emphasised, and, in the second, emphasis is being given to the date itself. In both cases, the sentences actually sound more interesting. To have the prepositional phrases at the beginning also creates a climax.

> Remember this in your own writing: variety of structure by re-positioning prepositional phrases can be an effective way of arresting the reader's attention!

Subordinate clauses, lists, parallel structure, climax

Subordinate clauses can also be used very effectively in your own writing. Remember that the positioning of subordinate clauses at the beginning of sentences can be a marker of more formal prose. Look at the following sentence, part of an article by Simon Firth in the *Sunday Herald*, on the effect of the Live Aid concert in 1985 on music and television, and how they both interact to make money today:

> Twenty years later, reflecting on what has happened since to music and television, to charity and Africa, to Bob Geldof and politics, I suddenly wonder if the media were not being remarkably prescient after all.

There is a long subordinate clause at the beginning of that sentence: *Twenty years later, reflecting on what has happened since to music and television, to charity and Africa, to Bob Geldof and politics.* Note also the author's use of the **list** in **parallel structure**: *to music and television, to charity and Africa, to Bob Geldof and politics,* again, in this case, another feature of the formality of the prose. It is worth noting that the sentence is all the more interesting and also dramatic because the main point – *if the media were not being remarkably prescient after all* – is delayed to the end, creating a **climax**. (*Prescient* means knowing events before they take place.) Moreover, the parallel structure gives the sentence rhythm, which makes the reader pay attention to meaning.

Again from the same article, note the placing of the subordinate clauses at the beginning of the following sentences:

> When I watch the Live Aid show, Freddie Mercury's performance seems the most remarkable. What I have come to realise is that he, more than any other acts, knows what is involved in selling himself, not just to the Wembley crowd, but to the television audience.

The main clause in the first sentence is *Freddie Mercury's performance seems the most remarkable*: in this case, it makes sense to place the subordinate clause at the beginning, but it also creates that stylish effect. What is interesting about the second sentence is the insertion of *more than any other acts* as a **parenthesis**, which helps delay the main point *knows what is involved in selling himself, not just to the Wembley crowd, but to the television audience* to the end, building up to the climax – *but to the television audience*.

All these are techniques to use in your own writing in order to give it variety and style.

Short and long sentences

The use of short and long sentences is another technique by which you can add variety to your prose and also create dramatic impact.

Look at these sentences from *Regeneration* by Pat Barker. The novel is set in 1917, at Craiglockhart, Edinburgh, a place where shell-shocked soldiers were sent to recuperate from the trench warfare of the First World War, in 1917. In one scene, a character, Burns, is standing by the window of his room, thinking about taking a bus out of Edinburgh to escape for a while:

> *A sharp gust of wind blew rain against the glass. Somehow or other he was going to have to get out. It wasn't forbidden, it was even encouraged, though he himself didn't go out much. He got his coat and went downstairs. On the corridor he met one of the nurses from his ward, who looked surprised to see him wearing his coat, but didn't ask where he was going.*
>
> *At the main gates he stopped. Because he'd been inside so long, the possibilities seemed endless, though they resolved themselves quickly into two. Into Edinburgh, or away. And that was no choice at all: he knew he wasn't up to facing traffic.*

Look at the number of short sentences, which add dramatic impact beside the longer ones, especially before the long final sentence of the first paragraph. Also interesting is the short sentence at the beginning of the second paragraph, again contrasting with the long last sentence of the previous paragraph. It not only creates drama, but it also creates pace – the short sentences convey the man's panic to the reader. Note also the dramatic effect of the sentence beginning with *And*.

For some reason, we are taught in our early years never to begin a sentence with *And*, yet that can be a very effective way of beginning a sentence, as is the case here. Look at this next example where a sentence begins in an unusual way. It is from an article in *The Guardian* by Alistair Cooke. He had been describing the extreme care taken by Wells Fargo, a security company, when collecting vast sums of money from various organisations to take to the bank. These are his final two paragraphs:

> *The money bags are marked and carried by the security men to a guard who was locked in the truck on its arrival. The guard signals that all is well to the driver, who climbs aboard, pausing only to check his sidearms. The truck takes off on the long drive to Wall Street, where the bags are lifted across the sidewalk under the watchful eye of the armed truck crew and two receiving guards, alerted by an electronic buzz as soon as the truck stops outside.*
>
> *In fact, you could say that the only time the money bags are flashed in public is on their brief passage across the sidewalk in front of the Morgan Guaranty Trust Co. at 23 Wall Street. Which was where, last Wednesday, three agile young men grabbed them and made off with a total swag of one million, three hundred and seventy-seven thousand dollars.*

Look at the final sentence. It begins with a relative pronoun – *Which* – and that is most unusual because a relative pronoun agrees with its antecedent – in this case, *the brief passage across the sidewalk in front of the Morgan Guaranty*

Trust Co. at 23 Wall Street. But the effect is comic, especially with the insertion of the phrases *last Wednesday* and *three agile young men grabbed them and made off* which has the effect once again of climax: the joke is delayed to the very end of the sentence. Note also that $1,377,000 is written in words, which also makes the joke more effective because it sounds so much more.

Link sentences

Another important aspect of all writing is to ensure that your piece is cohesive: that is, the paragraphs should be linked in such a way that the piece 'hangs together' as one unit. Note in the above example that Alistair Cooke uses *In fact* to link the paragraphs.

> Link sentences are especially important in discursive, formal writing since they enable the line of thought to flow more easily, thus allowing the argument to be developed effectively.

Use of colon and semi-colon

As we have already noted, the semi-colon is an underused, underrated punctuation mark. Not only does its use make your writing appear stylish, it is actually very helpful in indicating a connection between two units of sense. Often, you can avoid the comma splice by using the semi-colon.

The colon is useful for the introduction of lists and explanations. Again, it is a stylish punctuation mark.

Imagery, tone, word choice

The problem with much writing is that very often it is **clichéd**: the writer uses tired, worn-out metaphors that we have all heard too often before. Try to use original expressions, original images. Laurie Lee, in *Cider with Rosie* describes two friends as *limpet chums*, a vividly original and therefore effective expression which captures perfectly their closeness both emotionally and physically – clearly, the chums were never apart.

Look at the following extract from Clive James's book, *The Crystal Bucket*, a collection of pieces from his time as a television columnist for *The Observer* newspaper. In the excerpt below, James considers the impact made on the viewer by the original series of *The Incredible Hulk*:

> *Hulk has a standard body-builder's physique, with two sets of shoulders one on top of the other and wings of lateral muscle that hold his arms out from his*

sides as if his armpits had piles. He is made remarkable by his avocado complexion, eyes like plovers' eggs and the same permanently exposed lower teeth displayed by Richard Harris[1] when he is acting determined, or indeed just acting.

Given a flying start by the shock effect of his personal appearance, Hulk goes into action against the heavies, flinging them about in slow motion. Like Bionic Woman, Six Million Dollar Man and Wonderwoman, Hulk does his action numbers at glacial speed. Emitting slow roars of rage, Hulk runs very slowly towards the enemy, who slowly attempt to make their escape. But no matter how slowly they run, Hulk runs more slowly. Slowly he picks them up, gradually bangs their head together, and with a supreme burst of lethargy throws them through the side of a building.

[1] Richard Harris – an actor famous in the 1970s and 1980s and more recently in the Harry Potter films.

The paragraphs sparkle with originality. There is running throughout a gentle **sarcasm** mocking the programme. Expressions such as: *two sets of shoulders one on top of the other* and *wings of lateral muscle* and *that hold his arms out from his sides as if his armpits had piles* contribute to the sarcastic tone because they create such ridiculous images – the juxtaposition of *armpits* and *piles*, for example, is as witty as it is outrageous. Clive James is using the language to create original witticisms, avoiding **clichés** and worn-out jokes. The expression, *Hulk does his action numbers at glacial speed*, is particularly effective because *glacial speed* is an **oxymoron:** glaciers, however they may move, do not move at speed! Yet the image captures so accurately television's obsession (still there to this day) with using slow motion to portray violent action that could only in reality take place quickly.

The repetition of the notion of slowness in the last paragraph is highly effective because James does not just repeat the word *slowly* but develops the idea with words such as *gradually* and *lethargy*.

> Rule: avoid at all costs clichéd writing and images that are as limp and wet as yesterday's lettuce.

THE VARIOUS TYPES OF WRITING

Let's take a close look at each of the types of writing outlined at the beginning of this Chapter:

Personal/reflective writing

Many candidates are most comfortable with the Personal Essay, partly because they think that it is the most straightforward to produce, but what you have to ensure is that your piece is more than the retelling of an experience – you have to display the ability to reflect on the experience. Furthermore, don't try to produce some great dramatic event; use a fairly simple experience, but give plenty of personal detail in such a way that you imply the effect that it had on you. You should also consider symbolism to represent some of the aspects of the experience about which you are writing.

Whatever, avoid producing a rambling, witless **anecdote**. There is nothing more boring than a story that has neither wit nor point: give your story shape and ensure that it is reflective.

Discursive writing

> Most people think that this is the most difficult type of writing and, while it is not easy, you have to remember that you have to produce two discursive essays – the Critical Essays – under exam conditions.

The essays you produce for the Critical Essay are discursive in that you are presenting an argument or line of thought. Since a discursive essay is an essay where you set out an argument, you have to muster the skills of marshalling ideas and thoughts, presenting them in a logical sequence, and then expressing them in precise, formal prose.

If you are going to tackle the discursive essay try to steer away from clichéd topics such as animal rights, or euthanasia, or fox hunting. If you must tackle one of these subjects try to present it from a different angle. Better still, write about something that really interests you and about which you know you can engage your reader's interest.

Creative/imaginative writing

Normally we think of a short story when we think of creative writing, but it need not be restricted to the short story format – you can produce a piece of prose fiction which is an extract from a novel. You can produce a poem or a dramatic script, such as a monologue, a short scene, or a sketch. If you decide to produce a short story, try not to choose a subject about which you know nothing. And do remember the format of the short story: few characters, a simple plot, best based on your own experience, and a resolution which will make the reader think – or, at least, smile!

Persuasive writing

Persuasive writing is not unlike discursive writing in that you choose a subject about which you feel very strongly, though unlike discursive you do not need to present a carefully constructed argument. Nor do you need to take account of counter arguments. You do need, however, to use the language of persuasion to coax, or even cajole, your reader to your point of view. For those of you already skilled with language, the persuasive essay could be an excellent choice.

17 Avoid These Mistakes

Common errors

Other mistakes and confusions to avoid

Even the most talented of writers make mistakes. English is a highly complex language and it is almost impossible to write it without error. That is why you have to check carefully what you have written.

COMMON ERRORS

The following are the most commonly made errors, which, of course, you must avoid.

The comma splice

The inability to use the comma is one of the most worrying aspects of modern written English. Letters from bank managers, from solicitors, from directors of council services, even from civil servants abound with comma splices. One of the most frequent mistake is brought about by those who think that *however* is a conjunction. For example, an extract from a fictitious but not untypical (note the litotes!) bank manager:

> *Bank of Banchory's policy is to give every customer a protected overdraft, however, you must not exceed the agreed limit.*

How can you take such a bank seriously! A full stop or a semi-colon after the word *overdraft* would correct the error. Remind yourself of what we said about the Comma Splice on pages 56–57.

The absence of a comma

The following sentence is not easy to read because the author has omitted the comma after the opening phrase:

> *To begin with a photograph has a direct physical relationship with its subject.*

The comma after *with* makes all the difference – see what is meant about punctuation helping the reader?

Punctuation of direct speech

Again, many candidates cannot punctuate direct speech. Rather than point out errors, here are the conventional guidelines for the punctuation of direct speech:

- The words actually spoken are surrounded by inverted commas:

    'Hello, George, how are you?'

- Note that the question mark is placed **inside** the inverted commas.
- You need a new paragraph for each new speaker or the words leading up to a new speaker. Here is the extract from *Heart Songs* again:

    She was also getting tired of being broke, getting close to sniffing out Snipe's longing for a gutter.

    'You got a job, I hope,' she said.

    'Ahhh,' said Snipe, grinning like a set of teeth on a dish, 'there really wasn't any job after all. We just played. But some very fine country stuff.'

Had there been a question mark after *I hope*, it would have gone **inside** the inverted commas. Note also that the second part of Snipe's speech begins with lower case *'there really wasn't...'* because the sentence begins in the first part with *'Ahhh'* and continues with *'there really wasn't.'*

Variation in sentence structure

Try not to use a string of monotonous simple sentences. Vary your sentence structure using a combination of long and short sentences and use subordination. For example, begin sentences with *Although* or *Since* or *However much you feel that...* Variety means that the reader is less likely to be bored!

Number agreement

In English, the pronoun agrees in number with the preceding noun. For example, in the sentence:

- The boy ate his apples.

The word *his* agrees in number with the word *boy*. That is, because *boy* is singular, so the word *his* has to be singular. This is not the case in other languages. For example, translate that same sentence into French:

- Le garçon a mangé ses pommes.

Although the word *garçon* is singular the word *ses* is plural because the pronoun agrees in number with the word following.

So what? Does that matter? you may well ask. Well, it does matter in English. With the word *boy* there is no problem because the word is clearly masculine – they are *his* apples. The problem arises when the preceding noun is not obviously masculine or feminine. If the sentence were:

- The *person* ate his apples.

it would be grammatically correct but we would object because the word *his* is sexist. Fifty years ago, it was accepted that the words *he* and *his* could be used to represent both the masculine and the feminine, but since that is no longer the case English has a problem. To be grammatically accurate, we should write:

- The person ate his/her apples

but that sounds awkward and clumsy. One newspaper tried to introduce the pronoun *hir* to overcome the problem:

- The person ate *hir* apples.

For fairly obvious reasons that coining did not catch on. People now tend to use the plural *their* to overcome the problem – *The person ate their apples* – but clearly *their* is plural and *person* is singular. Perhaps it is best to avoid the construction in the first place.

A glaring example of what I mean is the message you hear when you dial British Telecom 1471 service. If you have been called by a withheld number, the announcer tells you:

- *The caller withheld their number*

Clearly *caller* is singular and *their* is plural. Better to have said: *The number was withheld by the caller.*

Other examples of number agreement

Words such as 'no-one', 'none' and 'anyone' are singular and take a singular verb:

- None of us *is* going to the party; and
- No-one *was* there.

Watch out for singular nouns that look plural. For example, which is right:

- *A pair of scissors is what you need* or *A pair of scissors are what you need*?

Though *pair* and *scissors* feel as though they are plural, nevertheless in this context *A pair of scissors* is a singular item, therefore *A pair of scissors **is** what you need* is correct.

In English number is not that straightforward – so just be alert. We have already looked at how English forms the plural on pages 54 and 55. But number is not always the same as singular/plural. For example, the word *rabbit* looks and is singular. The plural is formed regularly by adding an *–s*. Easy enough? *Rabbits*, then, is the plural. So, *We have two rabbits* is correct. But what about *We have been shooting rabbit all day?* That does mean something different from *We have been shooting rabbits all day!* If we think of the rabbits as lots of little furry individuals all being shot, then we use the plural *rabbits*; but if we think of them as category – like reindeer and duck – then we use the singular. It is the same with meat. You don't ask the butcher for *some porks*: you ask for *pork*. Yet, although we say *I should like two steaks please* we also say *I should like some steak*. English is complicated!

OTHER MISTAKES AND CONFUSIONS TO AVOID

Plural nouns with singular verbs

Another common error today is the use of the singular verb associated with a plural noun. Even the most educated people have been heard to say *There's two of them* and that is wrong. *There are two of them* is quite correct.

Fewer and less

One final point about number: it is not so much a confusion between the words *fewer* and *less*, it's that the word *less* is taking over and being used wrongly. *Fewer* should be used with numbers and *less* with categories or concepts.

For example:

- There were fewer than eight people in attendance; and
- There was less petrol in the car than I expected

are both correct, whereas:

- Express Checkout: for customers with less than nine items

is quite wrong – **fewer** *than nine items* is the right expression.

The following are correct:

- There were *fewer* dogs in the kennels than yesterday.

- That recipe calls for *fewer* tomatoes.

But you might say:

- There were less than a hundred at the concert

because 'a hundred' can be thought of as a concept. You would, however, have to say:

- There were fewer than nine people at the concert.

Imply and infer

These two words are often confused nowadays. *Imply* means what is intended by a text whereas *infer* is the deduction the reader makes from the text. For example, *this letter implies that you have won a great deal of money* but *I infer from the letter that my offer has been accepted.* Or: *What are you implying?* but *I infer from your attitude…*

Disinterested and uninterested

Again these words get confused. *Disinterested* means unbiased or objective whereas *uninterested* means bored. For example, a disinterested person has no axe to grind, and is someone who has no expectation or interest in the outcome of an event whereas someone who is uninterested is someone who is bored with the event. I am *uninterested* in Reggie, but when it comes to politics I am a *disinterested* observer.

Like and such

You cannot really say: *Someone like my friend* since there is no-one **like** your friend – he or she is unique. You should say: *Someone such as my friend.* You can however say: *He is like his father* because you are making a direct comparison.

Waiting on and waiting for

You should try to remember that *waiting on* refers to what a waiter does – he or she *waits on* a table whereas *waiting for* refers to the process of waiting for something to happen. Therefore, you can say: *The diner was getting impatient waiting for the young man to wait on his table.* It sounds inelegant but it is correct!

Different from

There is a tendency – probably leaking from America – for people to say *different to*. This usage is quite wrong. Even a respectable phone company has in one of its recorded messages – *The following menu may now be different to the one you are used to*. Of course it should be *different **from** the one you are used to*.

Alternatives and possibilities

Since *alternative* comes from the Latin *alter* meaning *one or other of two*, it should not be used when a choice involves more than two. For example, *There are three alternatives* is wrong – it should be *There are three possibilities*.

Between and among

Again *between* technically can only apply when two items or persons are involved, otherwise we should use *among*. Thus: *Between the two of us* is correct and *Among the three of us* is also correct.

All right

Despite the titles of television shows, the word *alright* is still highly informal. It is better to use *all right* – two separate words!

Split infinitive

It has always been regarded as bad form to split an infinitive (*to go*, *to jump*, *to swim*) in English. English grammar was traditionally based on Latin grammar, and because the infinitive in Latin cannot be split – e.g. *ducere* (to lead), *amare* (to love), it was felt that you should not insert anything between, for example, the *to* and the *go* of the verb *to go*. The pattern was broken by *Star Trek* with its famous *To boldly go...* I still think, however, you should be careful about splitting an infinitive, simply because the word inserted (invariably an adverb) throws too much emphasis on that adverb. For example, while *to boldly go* is perfectly acceptable (*to go boldly* has not the same effect), nevertheless *to desperately seek* does not work since there is too much emphasis on the adverb *desperately*.

Credence/credibility

There is an increasing confusion of these two words: even educated writers are using *credence* when they mean *credibility*. The word *credence* simply means *belief* or *acceptance* as in *There can be no credence to that evidence* whereas *credibility* means *that which is capable of being believed* as in *His story has no credibility*. The distinction is subtle but important.

Due to/owing to

Owing to is largely being replaced by *due to*, sadly. *Due to* means *caused by* and *owing to* means *on account of*, therefore a shop notice such as *Due to illness, the shop will be closed today* makes little sense because shops can't be ill! The notice should read: *Owing to illness, the shop will be closed today*. You can of course say: *Due to illness, I shall be unable to attend the meeting*.

The difficulty of English

As I said before – English is a highly complex language and it is easy to make mistakes. But if you are aware of the kind of errors and/or confusions that I have listed above, you can improve your writing enormously! There is nothing worse than an educated person making the most elementary mistakes in written English.

It may seem a bit pedantic to regard some of the mistakes/confusions I have pointed out above as serious, but when it comes to your CV or an application form, it can be crucial that you write correctly and accurately, with no infelicities of style or solecistic errors! Check those two words out!

In any case, it seems a shame to lose useful shades of meaning!

Conclusion

I hope that this book has taught you a great deal about words, sentence structure, punctuation, paragraphs, paragraph linkage, narrative structure, imagery and other literary devices. I also hope that not only will you avoid solecisms in your written English but that your prose style will vibrate – nay, coruscate – with original and apt imagery.

But I also hope I have gone further than dealing with technique alone. The technicalities of language are only the methods by which meaning is expressed: after all, alter the form of a sentence and you alter its meaning. Remember?

But it is not only sentences that have meaning. All literature is invested with meaning – themes, issues, areas of experience to be investigated and explored. Even *Coronation Street* portrays issues that affect us either socially or personally, no doubt informing some aspect of human relationships. How much more, then, does *Hamlet* or *The Crucible* or *The Whitsun Weddings* comment on and interpret our experience? And the process is two-way: we have to take our experiences to the text in order to make sense of it and, at the same time our experience is thereby heightened and illuminated and our understanding enlightened and enhanced.

I trust that this book has helped you improve your reading skills and that you regard all literature as something more than a task to be endured in order to pass exams. Literature is not like some geometric theorem that has to be conned by rote and regurgitated at will. Our greatest poets, novelists and dramatists did not really have Higher English in mind when they penned some of the most inspiring masterpieces of all time. Literature is there to be enjoyed, not just for its own sake, though that is important, but for what it tells us about our human condition.

ANSWERS

Chapter 3 – page 23

1	Mary had a little lamb	– **main clause**
2	I saw a ship on the horizon	– **main clause**
3	As the train slowed	– **subordinate clause**
	I gathered together all my luggage	– **main clause**
4	English is my favourite subject	– **main clause**
	Because it is so fascinating	– **subordinate clause**
5	I wandered lonely as a cloud	– **main clause**
	that floats on high o'er vales and hills	– **subordinate clause**

Chapter 4 – page 36

It is important to realise that the choice isn't between formal and informal: language use can vary from the extremely formal to the extremely informal. For Higher English purposes, however, as long as you understand these aspects of sentence structure then you will be able to recognise whether a sentence is formal or not.

1 Formal – **subordinate clauses** *When he replied quietly, with no shame or even shyness* and *that he had never really seen the sea* come at the beginning of the sentence.

2 Formal – **subordinate clause** *Although he had read the question paper for fifteen minutes* comes at the beginning.

3 Informal – there are no subordinate clauses.

4 Formal – **subordinate clauses** are at the beginning and the main clause *I see by their rapid eye movement that they must be asleep* comes at the end

Number 4 is an interesting case because the main clause looks as though it has a subordinate clause – *that they must be asleep* – attached to it, but really the normal word order would be *I see that they must be asleep by their rapid eye movement* – in which case *I see that they must be asleep* can be taken as one main clause. [This may seem odd since there are two verbs, therefore you would think two clauses, but because *I see* on its own doesn't really stand alone and make sense – it requires *that they must be asleep* to complete the sense: *I see* does not make sense on its own. This is a clear instance where grammar describes how the language is actually being used.]

Chapter 5 (first set) – page 35

1 There are two language features to note about this sentence:
   (a) the headword is *Deborah Winterbottom* and the word group *Anguished*

Answers

Coronation Street actress acts as a pre-modifier, a marker of informal English; and
(b) the absence of the definite article – *the* – before the word *Anguished* is another marker of informality. Formal English would include the word *the*: *The anguished actress*.

2. There are two language features to notice about this sentence:
   (a) the headword in the word group *A shock People investigation* is clearly the word *investigation*, and the newspaper title *People*, normally a proper noun, is here an adjective, which, along with the words *A* and *shock*, are pre-modifiers, a marker of informal, racy, tabloid style;
   (b) *top-class Rangers star* is also an expression pre-modifying *Freddie Sweet*, similarly indicating tabloid informality;
   (c) the definite article – *the* – has been omitted before *top-class*, another indicator of informality.

3. In this sentence the headword is *Dame Alison Campbell*, and the expression *one of Britain's most famous Shakespearean actresses* is clearly acting as a post-modifier, a marker of more formal prose. Those of you who have being paying close attention to this chapter will also note that the expression *one of Britain's most famous Shakespearean actresses* is in apposition to the headword.

4. In this sentence it is important to note that there is pre-modification – *Vicious, ten year old, clueless* – before the head word *tabby cat* followed by post-modification – *suspiciously named Earl Grey*. That amount of modification (pre and post) is an indication of the kind of informal English associated with tabloid press.

Chapter 5 (second set) – page 37

1. There is one prepositional phrase – *between these two islands* – which we can shift to the beginning of the sentence:

   Between these two islands, there is an unbelievably dangerous sweep of the river.

   The effect is to draw attention to the position of the dangerous sweep – it is between the islands.

   Also note that because we have altered the normal order by moving the prepositional phrase to the beginning of the sentence, there needs to be a comma inserted after the prepositional phrase.

2. In this sentence the prepositional phrase comes at the beginning of the sentence – let's shift it to the end and see the effect on meaning:

   It's easier to keep in touch with Mobile 50+.

   The word order is now in a normal sequence (hence no need for the comma) and the sentence no longer suggests that it's the Mobile 50+ that is important.

3. The next sentence has two prepositional phrases: *Yesterday* and *in the championships*. The emphasis is clearly on *when* the person ran rather than that he won.

   Yesterday, in the championships, I won the race.

Answers

We can alter this sentence in five ways:

(a) *In the championships, yesterday, I won the race.* In this case the event is emphasised.
(b) *Yesterday, I won the race in the championships.* Again, time is stressed though winning receives more emphasis than in the original sentence.
(c) *I won the race in the championships yesterday.* Normal word order, suggesting that winning is the important aspect of meaning.
(d) *I won the race yesterday in the championships.* Sounds odd because this is not quite the normal word order, yet it doesn't really emphasise any one aspect of meaning, apart from winning the race.
(e) *In the championships, I won the race yesterday.* Again, sounds odd – but more so – because the syntax of the sentence is being pushed towards the limits of meaning.

4 In this sentence, there are technically five prepositional phrases: *Along the canal bank, about twenty metres, from the towpath, just beneath the hawthorn hedge,* and *bordering the field,* though some could be taken as one prepositional phrase – e.g. *about twenty metres from the towpath* makes more sense as one prepositional phrase. To alter their position probably would not gain much, since the most important point is kept to the very end – *I saw the body.*

The obvious alteration would be:

I saw the body along the canal bank, about twenty metres from the towpath, just beneath the hawthorn hedge bordering the field.

But all the drama is lost!

Chapter 6 – page 42

Although the exam question allowed candidates to refer to *such language features as: word choice, sentence structure, tone, punctuation…* (and note that the **aposiopesis** means that the list of language features is not exclusive), nevertheless we will restrict ourselves to sentence structure alone. And it is perfectly possible to gain all three marks by referring only to sentence structure.

(a) The main clause comes at the end: *we have lowered our sights and reduced education to an assembly line* – and that creates **climax** and therefore a dramatic ending to the piece, the hallmark of an effective conclusion;
(b) There is the list that comes between the dashes. [Note that the paired dash – as in this case – is often a signal to the reader of **parenthesis**, normally classified as a device of punctuation; but since parenthesis is the isolation (between dashes, brackets, or even commas) of information that is additional to but not part of the grammar of a sentence then it is also a structural device.] Here we will treat the parenthesis – *our relationships with others, the quality of our friendships, our ability to be good parents, freedom to think for ourselves and to make choices, beauty, creativity, adventure, a sense of self worth* – as a feature of sentence structure, and note the **list** in **parallel structure,** where each item is increasing in length thus building up to a climax – *a sense of self-worth,* another feature of an effective conclusion;

Answers

(c) The **subordination** at the beginning of the sentence: *Instead of holding fast to a vision of what really matters*, and the list in parenthesis all delay the main point to the end, another feature of effective conclusions.

We have easily scored 3 marks!

Chapter 7 (first set) – page 51

1. The first thing to note is that the prepositional phrases *On June 16* and *in a move calculated to humiliate and frighten the Mexican people* come at the beginning of the sentence, thus delaying the main point (and main clause) *Cortez set fire to the aviaries* to the end – a clear example of climax which serves to dramatise the horror of setting fire to birds. The prepositional phrases also increase in length, further delaying and therefore adding to the climax and drama.

2. What is interesting about this sentence is that it comes in two parts, separated by a semi-colon. You still have to learn (in the next chapter) that one of the functions of the semi-colon is to signal a link in sense between the part of the sentence that precedes it and the part following the semi-colon. In this case, therefore, there is a link indicated between the letting go of the dog and its reactions at seeing the hanged man.

   [Please note that there are two versions of the verb *to hang*: *hung* is used for everything apart from people – for example, pictures are *hung*. But when it comes to people, we use *hanged* – for example, artists are *hanged*.]

   The *but* introduces a change: before the *but* the dog *galloped*, suggesting energy and fun, whereas after it the dog *stopped short, retreated*, and *looked out timorously* – suggesting suspicion and fear. Moreover, the **list** (*it stopped short, barked, and then retreated into a corner of the yard*) further draws attention to the movement and apprehension and the fear that the dog feels, building up to the climax and main point *looking timorously out at us*. The entire structure of the sentence reinforces the dramatic reaction of the dog and therefore reinforces the horror of capital punishment.

3. In this sentence, there are two prepositional phrases – *In one, sailors were singing at their work* and *in another, there were men aloft, high over my head, hanging to threads*, both of which build up to the climax *no thicker than a spider's*. The phrases also draw attention to and emphasise the sheer variety and amount of sailor activity. The sailors are clearly happy in their dangerous work.

4. In this sentence the most interesting aspect of structure is the list: *many old sailors, with rings in their ears, and whiskers curled in ringlets, and tarry pigtails, and their swaggering, clumsy sea-walk*. This time, note that the list is in polysyndetic structure, which has the effect of drawing attention to and dramatising each item in the list. The list also builds up climactically to the main point that the appearance of the sailors utterly delights the author.

5. This sentence is fairly easy to analyse: a list in parallel structure, building up to a dramatic climax. Also, the negative before *to yield* stresses the importance of not yielding!

Answers

Chapter 7 (second set) – page 52

In answering this question you have to quote the linking words in the sentence and demonstrate how they link to the ideas of the previous paragraph and the ideas developed in the current paragraph.

In this case the word 'these' links back to the issues outlined in the previous paragraph: that it is difficult to be sure that those after treasure or archaeologists can be prevented from exploring the site, that historic sites have always been plundered, that the site is so near to hydrogen wells and basalt mines. [It would be enough to say that the word 'these' links back to the issue of protecting the site from unwanted explorers.] The words 'convened a panel of 13 experts' links forward to the explanation of the kind of experts required.

Chapter 8 – page 56

the coat belonging to the boy	– the boy's coat
the scarf belonging to the girl	– the girl's scarf
the pullover belonging to the man	– the man's pullover
the cars belonging to the men	– the men's cars
the dresses belonging to the ladies	– the ladies' dresses
the ploughs belonging to the oxen	– the oxen's ploughs
the shoes belonging to the aliens	– the aliens' shoes
the tickets belonging to the senior citizens	– the senior citizens' tickets
the candy floss belonging to the children	– the children's candy floss
the money belonging to the bank manager	– the bank manager's money
the ship belonging to the captain	– the captain's ship
the computer belonging to the mother	– the mother's computer
the newspapers belonging to the men	– the men's newspapers

Chapter 8 – page 64

In this case, there are several points to be made about sentence structure:

(a) the parenthesis – (*men talk and discuss: women gossip, don't they?*), the effect of which is to draw attention to the irony;

(b) the addition of the question *don't they?* reinforces the irony;

(c) the repetition of *I see, I see, I rejoice* – creating a list building up to the climax of *the more women of our own age there are around us*;

(d) the pile up of adjectives – *thriving, gossiping and defiant* before the headword *sisterhood* – dramatises and therefore emphasises the author's point that it is her perception of the sisterhood that matters, not the social commentators'.

Answers

You should also refer to punctuation in your answer:

(a) the use of the colon in the parenthesis to create stylish, almost poetic, balance;
(b) the use of the inverted commas – *'growing social problem'*, which suggests irony. The inverted commas suggest that the author believes that it isn't a growing social problem, as others suggest.

GLOSSARY

Adjectives – describe a noun – as in *the black, dredger boat* where *black* and *dredger* are both adjectives describing the boat – see page 30

Adverbs – modify the verb – as in *Kevin walked across the road **slowly*** – slowly is the adverb which tells you *how* Kevin walked across the road – see page 32

Agnostic – someone who neither believes nor disbelieves in the existence of God – see page 83

Alliteration – a device of sound created by the repetition of consonants – see page 84

Allusions – reference in a text to other literary texts or to myths and legends or to the Bible – see page 67

Anecdote – a short story (sometimes within a longer narrative) that illustrates a point

Antecedents – the word or idea that has gone before the point being made – words such as *this, that, these, those* take antecedents – they should refer to something that has gone before – see page 47

Anti-climax – where in a list the least important item comes last, usually for comic effect

Aposiopesis – the three full stops at the end of a sentence indicating an unfinished idea or thought – see page 60

Apostrophe – the apostrophe is used to indicate possession – for example, *The girl's iPod* – or that a letter is missing, for example, *The boy can't work the iPod* – see page 55

Apposition – a form of post-modification, which agrees in number with the head word – see page 34

Assonance – a device of sound created by the repetition of vowels – see page 84

Asyndetic lists – a list which has no conjunctions between each item – as in *Go to the shops and buy me Hugo Boss aftershave, the new Philips electric razor, an Elizabeth Arden gift set, a Louis Vuitton bag* – see pages 44–45

Atmosphere – also referred to as tone and mood – tone/atmosphere/mood are created by word choice, imagery, and/or symbolism in order to enhance and support the ideas of the text – see page 112

Bathos – unintentional or accidental anti-climax – see page 83

Black humour – humour which explores the darker side of human nature, jokes about death, etc. – see page 83

Characterisation – the ways in which characters are established and developed, often used to portray the theme – see page 111

Higher English Grade Booster 151

Glossary

Clauses – a clause is a group of words containing one main verb – see pages 23

Cliché – a tired, worn-out phrase that has lost its meaning or effect – see page 134

Climactic structure – where the main point is delayed to the end of a sentence for dramatic effect – see page 41

Climax – see climactic structure – page 41

Coined – used to indicate that a word or word group (often a cliché) is being used in an unusual or ironic sense – as in *As the teacher said 'Nice to see you, to see you nice'* – see page 28

Colloquialism – informal language which is close to everyday speech – see page 77

Colon – the colon is used to introduce a list, to signal an explanation following a statement, to introduce a quotation, and to provide balance in a sentence – page 58

Comma splice – an error of punctuation, where the writer uses a comma to join (or splice) together two related units of sense – see pages 56–57. A semi-colon usually solves the problem.

Conclusion – the ending of a text, such that the ideas are brought together in a summative way – see pages 77–79

Conjunctions – linking and joining words – as in *and, because, but, since* – see page 32

Connotation – the associations we attach to any word – for example, *apple* suggests crisp, juicy, red, green, or Adam and Eve – pages 67–78

Context – the sentence in which a given word appears, such that the meaning of the word is made clear – sometimes the context can be the surrounding sentences – see page 67

Converting nouns to verbs – an American tendency to use nouns as verbs – *to goal, to trial, to text* – as in *He texted me yesterday*. See page 29.

Deconstruct – another term for analysis, where the critic deconstructs or analyses the way in which a text has been put together – see page 31

Definite article – the word *the* – see page 31

Denotation – the object in the universe to which a given word refers – see page 67

Dependent clause – another word for a subordinate clause

Dramatic irony – a feature of drama where the audience is aware of a situation, of which at least one other character is ignorant – see pages 85–86

Ellipsis – the three dots in the middle of a sentence to indicate that some words have been missed out – see page 61

Enjambement – a term used in poetry to describe run-on lines; where one line spills over into the next. Enjambement can also apply to run-on verses.

Flashback – a story which is told in a middle-beginning-end time structure

Foreshadowing – the use of symbolism, imagery, or an event at the beginning of a story which anticipates or suggests the development of the story – see page 82

Genre – the classification of literature: drama, prose, poetry (it also includes media studies)

Grammar – the classification of the way the language is put together

Groups – see Word Groups – see pages 33–36

Hyperbole – exaggeration for emphatic effect – see page 86

Imagery – a 'picture' which words create in your mind, such as 'a ship', 'a cat', a prince', but remember that an image can involve hearing, touch, taste and smell as well as sight

Imperative – that part of the verb that indicates command – for example, *Stop!* – see page 77

Indefinite article – the words *a*, and *an* – see page 31

Individual words – can be classified as nouns, verbs, adjectives, adverbs, etc. – see chapter 5 pages 29–32

Interjections – sounds which are inserted into a sentence to express emotion or surprise, etc. – as in *Oh!, Eh?, Woof!* see page 32

Irony – irony is a device by which the writer draws attention to meaning by apparently stating the opposite – irony has to involve a contrast in meaning and an implied comment – see page 85

Juxtaposition – the placing side by side of words or ideas

Linguistic devices – any device of language – see page 41

Linkage – the ways in which paragraphs are linked together to create a cohesive piece of writing – see page 47

List – a feature of sentence structure where the writer uses lists to create examples of the points being made: the effect can also be climactic – see pages 41 and 130–131 (see also parallel structure)

Literary – anything to do with literature – drama, novels, poetry

Literary devices – used to be referred to as figures of speech, such as metaphor, simile, metonymy – see chapter 10, page 80 onwards

Main clause – the main clause is the clause which stands alone and makes sense – as in *The new bride walked through the doors of the church which was on the top of the hill* – where *The new bride walked through the doors of the church* stands alone and makes sense, whereas the clause *which was on the top of the hill* cannot stand alone and is therefore a subordinate clause – see page 23

Metaphor – a device of comparison, where one thing is said to be another – see pages 70–72 and 80

Glossary

Metonymy – a device of representation, where one thing is said to represent the values or qualities of something greater than itself – for example, a rose can represent love – see pages 81–82

Minor sentence – a sentence without a verb – such as 'Yes.' or 'Well?'

Mood – also referred to as atmosphere and tone – tone/atmosphere/mood are created by word choice, imagery, and/or symbolism in order to enhance and support the ideas of the text – see page 112

Narrative structure – a narrative is any story and is structured in time with a beginning, middle, and end – the way in which the story is told is called the narrative structure: see chapter 13, pages 106–116

Narrative voice – the voice of the narrator as he or she relates the story

Nominal group – a group of words which act as a noun

Noun – the name of something – as in *boy, girl, telephone coffee, curtains* – see page 29

Onomatopoeia – a device where the sound of a word captures or reflects its meaning – for example, *Pow!, Crash!, Bang!* – see page 84

Oxymoron – the placing side by side of opposites – see page 82

Paragraph – a number of sentences grouped together to portray or explore a point or unit of sense – sometimes, for effect, a paragraph can consist of only one sentence

Parallel structure – a list which contains items in a repeated structure – for example, in the formula *to be + adjective (repeated)* or, most famously, *I came, I saw, I conquered* – see page 41

Parenthesis – a device which isolates information which is additional to a sentence but grammatically separate from it – see page 59

Parsing – identifying the parts of speech (or word classes) by means of their function – see page 27

Parts of speech – there are eight parts of speech (or word classes) noun, pronoun, adjective, verb, adverb, preposition, conjunction, interjection – but remember that a word should not be classified in isolation from its context – for example, you need to know the context to know whether the word *table* is a noun or a verb – see page 27

Personification – attributing human qualities to inanimate objects – see page 80

Phrase – a group of words which does not contain a verb – as in *The boy with the black eye*

Plot – a series of incidents causally related – see page 112

Point of view – the focus of the story on any particular character, whether in a novel or in some poems – remember the point of view can shift – see pages 109–110

Glossary

Polysyndetic list – a list which has conjunctions between each item – as in *Go to the shops and buy me Hugo Boss aftershave and the new Philips electric razor and an Elizabeth Arden gift set and a Louis Vuitton bag* – see page 44

Post-modification – the word group which comes after and describes the main or head word – as in *The new Audi TT convertible, with furry dice dangling from the interior mirror* – where *with furry dice dangling from the interior mirror* is an example of post-modification saying something about the car (or maybe its owner!) – see page 33

Prefix – the element which is attached to the front of a stem (or root) word – for example, *dis*appear – see page 66

Pre-modification – the group which comes before and describes the head or main word – as in *The tall, dark-haired, bearded police officer* where *The tall, dark-haired, bearded* is an example of pre-modification describing the police officer – see page 33

Prepositional phrase – a phrase which begins with a preposition – as in, *at the cinema, in the morning, in France, by the sea* – see page 35

Prepositions – words which indicate relationships between objects – as in *under, below, into* – see page 32

Present participle – the *-ing* word, suggests continuity of action – as in *Tess is **barking*** where *barking* tells us that the action is continuing – see page 31

Prolepsis – a device which anticipates an objection – as in *Before you say another word…* – see page 48

Pronoun – a word which stands for a noun – as in *he, she, it* – see page 30

Punctuation – the marks such as comma, full stop, colon, etc. which signal or clarify meaning

Relative pronoun – used after a noun to avoid repeating the noun – for example, *who, whose, which, that* – see page 30

Repetition – where words or phrases are repeated for emphatic effect – see page 40

Rhetorical device – a device associated with speeches, but not exclusively, intended to involve the listener (or reader) in what the speaker (or writer) has to say – for example, parallel structure – pages 47–48

Rhetorical question – a question where the answer is obvious or implied, used to draw the reader's attention to the point being made – see page 48

Rhythm – the use of alliteration, assonance, lists, repetition, and syllable stresses in order to create an emphatic and/or dramatic effect – see page 48

Sarcasm – where the writer states the opposite of what is meant in order to achieve ridicule – see page 86

Semi-colon – the semi-colon is used to separate complicated items in a complicated list; or to signal that two units of sense can be linked in the one sentence. A very sophisticated punctuation mark! – see page 58

Glossary

Semiotics – the study of signs or symbols – see page 112

Sentence – a sentence is a word or a combination of words which makes complete sense

Sentence structure – the arrangement of the words or word groups in a sentence

Setting – the place and time in which a story is set – see page 111

Signifiers – symbols which suggest a greater meaning, for example, lilies can be a signifier, but what they suggest to any one individual is the signified – i.e. lilies can symbolise peace or death – see page 112

Simile – a device of comparison, slightly weaker than metaphor, where one thing is said to be like another – page 80

Sound bite – a short, snappy, quotable expression much loved by politicians – see page 48

Spelling – it is important to be able to spell high frequency words accurately – see pages 65 and 66 for examples

Style – a writer's particular use of imagery, tone, anecdote, humour, word choice, sentence structure, punctuation, etc. to create a specific effect – see page 24

Subordinate clause – a clause which cannot stand on its own – as in *who climbed the mountain* – this clause makes no sense because it needs a main clause to support it, in other words it is subordinate to the main clause – see pages 24–25

Suffix – the element which is attached to the end of a stem (or root) word – for example, jump*ed* – see page 66

Symbolism – a device of representation where an object, idea, or logo represents something greater than itself – for example, a flag represents a country – see page 82

Synecdoche – a subset of metonymy where a part is used to represent the whole – for example, *They haven't even a roof over their heads* where *roof* is used to represent shelter – see page 82

Synonym – words which mean the same thing, such as 'taxi' and 'cab' – though each word has its own connotation (look up: connotation, pages 67–68)

Syntax – the way in which an individual sentence is put together

Tense – the ways in which we express time, such as present tense, past tense, or future tense

Theme – the issues or central ideas which the text explores – see page 111

Tone – also referred to as atmosphere and mood – tone/atmosphere/mood are created by word choice, imagery, and/or symbolism in order to enhance and support the ideas of the text – see page 112

Verb – the doing word – as in *to jog, to speak, to touch*, but also *to be* and *to have* – see page 31

Glossary

Vocative of address – where the writer addresses a person directly: for example, *Hello, George, how are you?* – George is said to be in the vocative of address – see page 58

Way paragraphs are linked – the opening sentence of a given paragraph should be linked to the ideas of the previous paragraph – no paragraph should exist in isolation

Word Choice – the words used in any given text to create effect or tone

Word classes – see parts of speech – see page 27

Word groups – where a group of words has a specific function – as in *The skateboarders with the hooded tops skated down the main stairs of the local library.* The word group *The skateboarders with the hooded tops* is the word group which performs the action (the nominal group) and the word groups *down the main stairs* and *of the local library* tell us where the action took place – see pages 33–35

Words – see parts of speech – see page 27

Acknowledgements

I owe an incalculable debt to several people: to Meg and Willie Cockburn, who also gave birth to my love for language, to my Head of Department at Dollar Academy, Billy Wilson (NED), who, in those heady days of the late 1960s, had a powerful and lasting influence on my understanding of grammar in particular and literature teaching in general; and to Tom and Alice Ferrie, with whom endless discussions about language helped clarify and develop my thinking. My gratitude to a former pupil of Dollar Academy, Alison Campbell, knows no limits. I must also thank Pappa Thomas for his unstinting assistance and motivation. I should like to pay tribute to the team at Leckie and Leckie, whose professionalism and care was a joy to experience. And, finally and most importantly, I should like to thank Kevin Bolton, without whose unswerving encouragement and support this book would never have been written.

Copyright acknowledgements

Leckie & Leckie is grateful to the copyright holders, as credited, for permission to use their material. Every effort has been made to trace the copyright holders and to obtain their permission for the use of copyright material. Leckie & Leckie will gladly receive information enabling them to rectify any error or omission in subsequent editions.

- Moira Andrew for the poem *Waiting Room* (pages 9, 39, 98, 119–120 and 122)
- The Independent for extracts from the article *Earthlings Keep Off* by Phil Reeves (pages 46, 70, 78 and 88)
- Enitharmon Press for an extract from *The Wasps' Nest* by George Macbeth (pages 102–103)
- The Guardian for an extract from an article by Alistair Cooke, copyright Guardian Newspapers Limited 1969 (pages 132–133)

The following companies/individuals have very generously given permission to reproduce their copyright material free of charge:

- The Scottish Qualifications Authority for extracts from examinations.
- Faber & Faber for a paragraph from *The Girl In Winter* by Philip Larkin (pages 24–25)
- Newsquest Media Group for extracts from the article *Can Britain Afford to Keep Talented Immigrants out?* by Ruth Wishart (pages 43, 45 and 89–90)
- Newsquest Media Group for extracts from the article *Is Paranoid Parenting the Greatest Danger to our Kids?* by Melanie Reid (pages 74, 89 and 92–93)
- William McIlvanney for an extract from *Surviving the Shipwreck* by William McIlvanney (page 50)
- Random House for an extract from *I'm a Little Special – A Muhammed Ali Reader* by Gerald Early (pages 62–63 and 68)
- Piatkus Books for an extract from *Growing Old Disgracefully: New Ideas for Getting the Most from Life* by Mary Cooper (page 64)
- HarperCollins for two extracts from *Heart Songs* by E Annie Proulx (pages 74 and 109–110)
- Random House for the poem *The Road Not Taken* by Robert Frost (pages 103–104)
- Penguin for an extract from *Regeneration* by Pat Barker (page 132)
- Macmillan UK for an extract from *The Crystal Bucket* by Clive James (pages 133–134)